Life is in Charge

A. Pearson

Life is in Charge

by

A. Pearson

Adelphi Press
4 - 6 Effie Road, London SW6 1TD

Copyright © 1993 A. Pearson

Printed and bound in UK
Typesetting by CBS Felixstowe Suffolk
Published by Adelphi Press
ISBN 1 85654 072 3

Contents

page

Introduction	
Life and Evolution	1
You	21
Men and Women	41
Marriage	81
Mankind	89
Our World in the Universe	99
Religion	107
Civilisations and Governments	121
Education	125
Pain	135
Contraception and Abortion	147
Genetic Engineering: Where will it End?	153
Television: Makes the Whole World Look Like	159
Newspapers and Red Herrings	165
Art, Painting, Sculpture: My Prejudices	169
Computers: Where Do We Go From Here?	173
Crime	175
War, Mass Murder: Will We Ever Stop?	183
Pornography	189
Death and Life: Quit Brooding About Death and LIVE	193

INTRODUCTION

This is a short trawl round a few of the things I think we know about ourselves and our world. The opinions and prejudices are all mine. You may disagree.

If you do, I suggest you write your own book.

It was Philip Larkin, the poet who said that "the only satisfactory book is the one you write yourself."

I have quoted from various people because they said what I wanted to say, but they said it better than I could.

I have given the authors where known but I have to apologise for not acknowledging anyone's copyright because my quotations are mainly taken from anthologies which have failed to acknowledge any copyrights.

CHAPTER I

LIFE AND EVOLUTION

"Life on Earth is like the bloom on a plum," says Lyall Watson.

I wish to proclaim a self-evident truth that everybody knows but nobody acknowledges.

We have all said at some time "Nature knows best" or "Leave it to Nature" or talked of "Mother Nature." Who and what do we mean by this "Mother Nature"? We can only mean LIFE itself. There is nothing else. We confuse the issue by referring to scenery as "Nature" when actually this refers to many of the obstacles that LIFE has to contend with. We do not know what LIFE is. We only know when it is present or when it is absent (most of the time, we cannot always be certain). If we plant seeds we only know if they are alive if roots form or leaves sprout.

LIFE ITSELF IS RESPONSIBLE FOR EVERYTHING ON THIS EARTH THAT LIVES.

LIFE DOES THE MAINTENANCE WITHOUT WHICH NOTHING COULD CONTINUE TO LIVE.

Of course this does not get us any nearer to solving the mystery of why we are all here, or why there is anything here at all, or what we are supposed to be doing here (beyond living) and what is the meaning of it all.

I doubt if we shall ever solve that mystery.

I know that all the millions of people who have been indoctrinated with one of the many religions now extant will not be able to acknowledge that LIFE is in charge and not the GOD that they have been brought up to believe in. Of course it will not make much difference to the great numbers of people who ignore all religions even now and who would rather not think about the Universe and their place in it.

We do not know where LIFE originated, but there is a theory that it came from outer space in cosmic dust, or meteorites. If this theory is correct then we must assume that there is LIFE somewhere else in the Universe and that Life has arrived all over the Earth at some time, and will go on arriving in the same way as long as there are conditions in which it can survive.

It may be as well if we never find LIFE on other worlds as it would only lead to galactic wars as in our scientific stories. We cannot live in peace with the inhabitants of this world let alone the people of another planet or world.

We have at times called LIFE God but we have imagined this God in man's image or the image of some animal. And when we call it God and make it in man's image we give it man's attributes because we know of no other.

In the Christian religion, the God of the Old Testament is a jealous God. It is a God who demands sacrifices. It is a God who desires material things like gold and precious stones just as man himself desires these things. It is a God who demands vengeance. It is a cruel God who destroys all the enemies of his chosen people. (And who has chosen them, they chose themselves through their priests)

In one instance, the God of Israel sent she-bears to destroy many small children who called one of his prophets 'baldhead' which he probably was, and which children have always done. A horrible revenge for a small offence.

Sometimes it is a God of love, but only to a chosen few. In fact this God is the epitome of a human being who has achieved tremendous power over other people, a tyrant in fact. And just to excuse his own evil behaviour, man, in the Christian religion has to invent a Devil who is responsible for tempting all mankind to wrong doing. And the Devil has all the attributes of a man. He may be delineated in all sorts of horrible guises, but when we look at some of LIFE'S creations we realise that our imaginations are nowhere compared to the creatures that LIFE has actually created. LIFE has anticipated our minds in every direction, and why not? We are after all LIFE'S creations ourselves.

All religions invented their own Gods. As Robert Ingersoll said: "An honest God is the noblest work of man."

Man makes his Gods mostly male, which in itself is ridiculous when we all know that the female of all plants and animals is the vessel of new life. Man makes Gods, who can, he thinks, he bribed and bargained with, just like their inventors. *"The Martyrdom of Man"* by W. Winwood Reade is a history of how man could have progressed from having many Gods to having just one in his religions.

Of course, if you believe in a personal God who has your well-being at heart I suppose you have no need to think how strange it is that we or anything else are on this planet Earth, one of the satellites of the Sun, a minor star on the edge of one of the millions of galaxies in the Universe. You are not overawed like the rest of us.

Somebody said that religion is usually the theory that the world was set spinning solely for us humans. M. Forest said, "It is sad that so many people appear to be interested in God because no-one is interested in them."

None of the Gods man has invented are big enough to be in command of the Universe. They have been little parochial Gods concerned only with a little corner of this planet Earth and only for a little while. What is 2,000 years in comparison with the millions of years that the Earth has existed?

Most of man's Gods were invented when we still thought that the Earth was the centre of the Universe and that the Sun went round the Earth. We did not know any better. Now we know more, but all new knowledge opens up another sea of ignorance. We shall never know it all, no matter how many space-ships we send, or how many telescopes we build, or wonderful microscopes we invent.

EVOLUTION

LIFE has always had to battle against the various climates, earthquakes, volcanoes, cosmic collisions and ice-ages, especially ice-ages as apparently the Earth has been covered by ice for much longer periods than it has been free from ice. Imagine yourself as LIFE creating living things on Earth.

Where do you start? You must use the same materials that the stars are made of. There are no others. You have to create things that are self-generating, self-healing, and have food for fuel to sustain them, and then you have to create other living things to clear up the debris, waste products, dead bodies etc. of the first creatures and so on *ad infinitum*.

After the seas were formed (from whence and why salty?) there is a theory that you started millions of years ago with proteins and nucleic acid to form molecules which were able to replicate themselves. You choose as your building blocks amino acids and electrical impulses. Then perhaps you created the single-celled bacteria that can live off sulphur and carbon dioxide, in an atmosphere of hydrogen, and a temperature probably near the boiling point of water, which were the conditions which probably existed on Earth before there was any oxygen.

Scientists have found the remains of the oldest-known Lifeforms on Earth, bacteria, 3• billion years old in Precambrian rock samples in north-western Australia. They look like modern bacteria. The scientists say that they are not perfectly preserved but they can see the cell walls. These bacteria have been found still living in the hot gases in volcanoes.

This must have been the first step that LIFE took, and then perhaps the one-celled plants in the seas which could feed on the worn-down rock sediments. They too had to be able to reproduce themselves, take in food and get rid of their waste products.

The next generation might have been free-floating one-celled organisms which could eat the one-celled plants, thus starting the food chain which runs through all living things until we get to mankind.

Mankind, perhaps LIFE's last creation so far, has opted out of the chain. He just eats everything else.

In all the theories of evolution that I have heard of, it seems that the proposers believe that everything evolves itself, and that all living things have done the evolving themselves into something different. Why should they have done that? How would they know how to do it? What possible motive could they have?

There are some that have not evolved. They are still here.

In the excellent T.V. series 'Life on Earth' and in the same book by Sir David Attenborough, the probable progression of Life's creations are briefly described and beautifully photographed, but it is implied that land animals evolved from water animals because some decided to walk on land. I cannot think that this is a probable progression, because if conscious thought could evolve the structure of any animal, man would have evolved himself a second pair of eyes in the back of his head, a second pair of arms; probably another sitting position; a respiratory system apart from eating and drinking so that we should never choke, and as for sex, well, you choose your own improvements or modifications. And certainly self-generating limbs and renewable hair and teeth such as some animals already have. (Perhaps we were once able to generate lost limbs. According to a report once in *The New Scientist* about Hallam Hospital, children who had lost the ends of their fingers and who did not have the ends sewn up, found that the finger tips regenerated with even the finger prints intact. Also a boy appeared on T.V. in 1987 with a new grown top-joint of his thumb after amputation following an accident. Some sort of electrical treatment had been used.)

For evolution to take place there must be some driving force otherwise everything would stay as it was. We know that some that have been around in fossil form millions of years ago, are still here as living plants, animals and insects. The force that makes them change must be LIFE itself. There is no other.

Many of LIFE'S animals and insects are built in the same sort of pattern, with eyes (where needed) ears, mouths, blood pumps, digestive systems, outer skin, bony structure, inside or outside etc. The variations are endless. If they had all evolved in the same way at the same time the fossil plants etc, would not still be around.

Everything in the food chain must taste good to the ones who eat it. If everything evolved itself, would it ensure that it tasted good to its enemies? Would it indeed?

There is a theory that I think is very foolish, that everything evolved by blind chance. If that is correct where are the inbetween stages, or the fossils of the inbetween stages.

There are none of course, because if an animal grew an extra claw or whatever, it would have to grow the nerves, muscles and brain connections to operate the new growth. Parts grown by blind chance would not be much use hanging around for millions of years awaiting chance connections.

There have not been enough millions of years in which all the millions of different species we know about to have appeared by blind chance, let alone all the species that probably disappeared during the various ice-ages. Just how many blind chance alterations would there have to be between a butterfly and a rhinoceros?

Also every living thing is exactly tailored to the life it has to lead, in the climate in which it finds itself. If the climate changes too suddenly it either moves elsewhere or dies. Perhaps LIFE is keeping the singe-celled organisms to start all over again when man has destroyed himself and many of LIFE'S creations. But in all probability far more of LIFE'S creations have been destroyed by floods and ice-ages than man has ever destroyed. This is, of course no reason why man should go on destroying any species.

Palaeontologists suggest that around 250 million years ago up to 96% of all species on Earth became extinct, not all at once but over a period of a few hundred thousand years, at a time when all the continents may have been united as one large continent. Some have suggested that it was an ice-age that caused this calamity, but others suggest that for various reasons oxygen became in short supply and carbon dioxide increased so that most of the marine life and most of the land animals gradually disappeared because there was not enough oxygen to keep them alive, so they suffocated. Is this what is likely to happen to all the living animals on the Earth and in the seas in the future?

We cannot perceive LIFE actually creating new creatures right now but it may still be going on. There are reputed to be thousands of plants, birds and insects that man has never seen in the forests of the Amazon and elsewhere, and as the forests are being destroyed no-one will ever see them.

It is thought that LIFE is altering the chemistry of mosquitos so that they have become immune to D.D.T and other poisons which have been used in an attempt to eliminate them. It is the female mosquito which needs blood (animal or human) to produce her eggs. She is the carrier of malaria from one victim to another in her spittle when she penetrates the skin. Again, the attempt to get rid of rats by "Warfarin" which prevents the blood from clotting so that the rats bleed to death, has not eliminated them. They flourish in ever greater numbers.

This form of rat poison is now used by humans, not to poison them, but to thin down the blood when it is too viscous.

We know that LIFE can cause chemical changes in plants and animals when certain elements are deficient.

In Canada, somewhere near Banff, high in the Canadian Rockies there is a small quarry called the Burgess Shale where fossils have been found of soft-bodies small animals which are thought to have been preserved by sudden mud slides excluding oxygen. These animals apparently bear no resemblance to any other known animals and probably became extinct some 550 million years ago.

This shows that LIFE has started all over again with different models at various times. There are probably many other types of animals that LIFE invented and that we shall never know about because their fossils have not been preserved when for some unknown reason they became extinct.

BACTERIA ARE THE FOUNDATION OF ALL LIFE

Some bacteria help animals to digest cellulose as do those in the stomachs of cows and other animals. Some bacteria purify drinking water. Some live in animals and humans and prevent their bodies from breaking down. Some, like yeasts cause fermentation and we use them to make cheese and alcohol etc. Some break down garden rubbish into compost. More could be used to recycle more of the man-made rubbish.

Everything that lives can be recycled. Nothing is wasted. We can see this when we consider the terrible crude oil which is spilt all over the world, and which has had a devastating effect on the flora and fauna of so many coastlines. After a while, perhaps a few years, the oil will have completely disappeared. It is only man-made rubbish that persists. But why LIFE created bacteria and viruses that cause disease is another mystery that we shall never solve.

Remember, do not despise the single-celled organisms. You were one yourself once!

You are one of LIFE'S miracles. Miracles are not conjuring tricks of turning water into wine. Consider LIFE'S miracle of turning a woman's egg, no bigger than the head of a pin, invaded by a single sperm too small to be seen with the naked eye, into you. One cell becomes millions, all seemingly making decisions to become an arm or a leg or a brain, etc. etc. until when you are complete with the mechanism to breathe air for the first time you decide to be born. Because this happens millions of times resulting in millions of people, it is no less a miracle every time. Think of caterpillars turning into butterflies, tadpoles turning into frogs and all the other daily miracles, including seeds pollinated by the wind or insects which turn into plants and trees. Some seeds are as fine as dust but each carries its own programme of what it should become. But the biggest miracle of all is that LIFE came to this planet.

Some of the earlier of LIFE'S organisms seem to have propagated themselves by budding bits off (how?) with each bit having a nucleus. Then LIFE created two sexes.

Now, (until man's intervention, cuttings and clones etc,) no two living things would ever be exactly alike. They would all be random. Not in their shape or form, but in that choice of which pollen grain will alight on which pistil is random, and the animal or human egg will be fertilized by the first sperm to reach the egg and penetrate its outer shell, is random. So no-one can foretell which characteristics of which plant or animal will be transmitted. Deaths too, are random. No-one can tell foretell which will die and which will live and for how long (except, of course, when man deliberately destroys people, plants and animals.)

LIFE may have created the multi-celled organisms after the single-celled organisms. These may have been plants in their infinite variety reproducing themselves from seeds from flowers, and at first cross-pollinated by the wind as some still are.

The earlier plants still with us, can only be grown from seeds, and not cuttings. The Ginko tree is supposed to be such an early example.

When LIFE created flowers that had to be pollinated by insects instead of the wind, LIFE must have created the insects at the same time. Why produce nectar in flowers such as honeysuckle to attract insects to feed on the nectar while pollinating the flowers, unless the insects were already there? Brightly coloured flowers were created to attract insects as were sweet smells (or in some cases rotting flesh smells). Plants and flowers have no brains and no eyes as far as we know, so how do they know how to attract the right sort of insects to carry the male element, the pollen to the female element, the pistil (leading to the ovary where the seeds are produced) of other flowers of the same variety to cross pollinate them? The flowers themselves do not know. It is LIFE that is in charge and arranges it all.

Some time ago there was a very good T.V. programme called, I think 'The Sex Life of Plants and Flowers'. It illustrated with beautiful photographs the myriad ways in which plants trap insects into pollinating them, and how the nectar tubes were tailored to the particular insect (or sometimes humming bird) most suitable for that plant.

How does the plant know how to do that? Some plants give out their perfume during the day to attract bees, wasps and insects, while others like honeysuckle produce their sweet-smelling scent at dusk to attract moths and late-flying insects.

How does the honeysuckle know when to produce its scent?

The variety I am writing about is scentless during the daylight hours. It cannot be the fading light which tells it, because if you cut a spray and put it in a vase in a well-lighted room it will produce its scent at the same time each evening as the honeysuckle growing in the garden.

I bought a white, jasmine plant from a chainstore. It was in flower in February, because it had been raised in a glasshouse. The leaves and flowers were exactly the same as the sweet-smelling garden variety which usually flowers in July. Because presumably there were only flies in the glasshouse to pollinate it the perfume of the February flowering plant had changed to a revolting smell which would attract the flies. How did the plant know that it should change its small?

The flowers of some orchids resemble the insects that they wish to do their pollinating. The genus Ophrey closely resembles female wasps, complete with eye spots and wings, and with the correct wasp smell. Male wasps try to mate with it and so are daubed with the pollen to pass on to the next bloom.

Other orchids mimic female tropical butterflies complete again with the right odour, thus attracting the pollinator they need. How do orchids know how to do this?

LIFE arranges it all, just as it arranges the camouflage of certain moths, snakes, fish etc, and bright red or yellow stripes or spots on insects and fish to indicate that they are not good eating, so defending them from their predators. But LIFE also gives this colouring to other insects and fish which are good eating so that they too may escape from their predators. But none of them escape every predator all the time. Eat and be eaten, that is LIFE'S law. All living things have been given two aims, to survive and breed. Mankind seems to have fulfilled both of these aims rather too well.

We do not know how LIFE keeps the balance between all living things (apart from mankind) if balance there is. We know that some animals, fish and turtles for example, lay thousands of eggs because very few will survive to maturity to produce the next generation. Most will become food for others. Butterflies lay a lot of eggs, many of which become caterpillars and food for birds. I doubt if the fish, turtle or butterfly knows why it lays so many eggs.

Many animals, insects and plants are provided with poisons to protect them from predators, but still some others are immune to these poisons so all eventually get eaten, and no one species seemed to prevail over all the others until man's arrival on the scene.

SURVIVAL OF THE FITTEST

I do believe in the survival of the fittest, the fittest to survive in the environment in which it finds itself. This is natural selection by LIFE.

We notice this in the animal world. The strongest male stags in the rutting season will collect a harem of females and challenge any other stag to take them away from him. The females choose him because he is the strongest and they want their offspring to survive. The same thing happens with seals; the biggest bull collects his harem and fights any other bull who tries to muscle in.

LIFE has fashioned all living things particularly to their environment. If the environment changes too suddenly, whatever it is may die. If the change is gradual LIFE will make the adjustments, to ensure that the plant or animal can continue to live.

On some islands, divided for perhaps millions of years from the mainland, some animals, insects, and plants will have become quite different from those on the mainland, probably because the climate has changed, or because maybe predators are absent. On islands where birds have no enemies some of them can no longer fly. They have no need if the food they prefer can be obtained without the effort of flying, which takes a lot of energy. Consequently, over the years their wings have tended to become too small for them to be able to fly.

We cannot know what has happened to that flightless bird, the ostrich. Did its long legs give it sufficient speed to outpace its enemies? Is it left over from the time of the dinosaurs? Or did it just grow too large?

Every living thing has a variable number of genes that ensure that some will live in fairly adverse conditions that will kill off others.

Some may be immune to diseases and some immune to chemicals etc, so that some of each species has a chance of surviving. Thus the environment or climate can cause a change in a species, because one is fitter to survive than another, and this can change one species into something slightly different.

We used to think that breeding between two different species always led to sterility. I am thinking of asses and horses breeding sterile mules. But now some mules are said to be fertile. We cannot tell how often it happens that two different species can give rise to another species but it must account for some of the many different species of birds, insects and animals there are in the world that we already know about. We have always thought of a species as one that could only breed with its own kind. But nowadays genetic engineering is producing some very peculiar crosses.

I am nowhere suggesting that LIFE created all the living things around to-day from scratch as it were. No, I believe that LIFE has evolved them to what they are (minus man's interventions) but, because of constant ice-ages and collisions of the Earth with other bodies, which have probably wiped out many of the previous plants and creatures, we are unable to trace an evolutionary path except perhaps from single-celled to multiple-celled organisms. There are probably no "missing links." We have not found any fossils of any, so we must assume that LIFE created each species as a separate creation.

MAN'S INTERVENTIONS

Despite his cleverness man has not yet discovered how to raise a column of water 400 feet effortlessly as any tree can to get water from its roots to its highest leaves. He has not yet made a computer that can store all the information needed to grow a fungus from a spore that weighs one sixth - hundred - billionth of an ounce. Plants are more efficient than even the most advanced of any of man's inventions. Man has used cross - fertilisation of plants to breed many different coloured and larger flowered plants than are found in the wild. Man even breeds some crosses between plants that LIFE does not seem to have produced. He also uses cuttings to ensure that future plants will be exactly alike when he is not able to control the fertilisation and production of identical seeds. But like the different shaped animals that man breeds (dogs, sheep, cows etc.) they would rarely survive for long in the wild, the plants because they usually revert to the original species, that being the fittest to survive in the jungle that is the wild, with every plant competing for space, food, and water against every other plant; and the animals will revert because they usually have difficulty giving birth without assistance. Man's works will last a very short time in Earth's time scale.

INSTINCT

We tend to describe the actions of all living creatures as

behaviour by instinct. What do we mean by instinct? One dictionary defines it as "a natural urge compelling a more or less definite mode of behaviour. Where does this "natural urge" come from? Why from LIFE itself. LIFE lays down the pattern so that all of its species can have a chance to live. Some eat one food and others another so that there is room for all until any species multiplies too fast and then their supply of food runs out and starvation cuts down the numbers.

EYES

Sir Isaac Newton wrote:

> "Whence is it that the eyes of all sorts of living creatures are transparent to the very bottom and the only transparent membrane in the body, having on the outside hard transparent skin, and within transparent humors, with a crystalline lens in the middle and a pupil before the lens, all of them so finely shaped and fitted for vision that no artist can mend them? Did blind chance know that there was light and what its refraction was, and fit the eyes of all living creatures (that needed eyes) after the most curious manner to make use of it? These and suchlike considerations always have and always will prevail with mankind to believe that there is a Being who makes all things." No say I, no being, but LIFE itself.

OUR ATMOSPHERE

As we do not know how our atmosphere originated we cannot know at which stage LIFE organised that animals and insects (apart from the volcano bacteria etc.) should breathe in oxygen and exhale carbon dioxide, and that plants should thrive on carbon dioxide, and give out oxygen.

There is theory that blue-green algae may have been the first plants to turn carbon dioxide into oxygen. Who knows? Nobody knows how the balance in the atmosphere is kept but if more plants and trees are destroyed and more of the Earth becomes desert, that balance is bound to be upset and oxygen become less abundant.

Also we are told that more carbon dioxide in the atmosphere from industry and fossil burning fuel used in automobiles could cause a greenhouse effect and make the atmosphere warmer, thus possibly melting the ice of the Polar regions which may in turn cause flooding of all the low-lying land of many countries. Of course there are many people who do not believe this theory. They think that the warming of the atmosphere could stave off the next ice-age.

On the other hand, if for any reason the oxygen in the atmosphere increased by a few percent, there is a belief that the Earth would become like a tinder-box and everything would go up in flames.

In one theory LIFE itself keeps the balance and regulates the atmosphere. It is thought that termites and other insects, and cows and sheep etc, produce methane which together with that produced by bacteria from rotting natural material is enough to destroy the excess oxygen and help to keep the atmosphere stable.

For some years there has been concern about large holes in the ozone layer of the atmosphere. These holes are said to be as large as the U.S.A. They seem to occur mainly over the Arctic and Ant-Arctic regions. As it is the ozone layer which filters out the ultra-violet rays from the Sun, so that little falls on the Earth, the disappearance of this layer could be responsible for skin cancers in anyone exposed to the Sun's rays at any time. One theory for the holes is the use of chlorines in the manufacture of fridges, cars and other goods and use of aerosols containing the chlorine gases which destroy the ozone.

Another theory is that planes flying above the Arctic and Ant-Arctic zones may have some deletrious effect.

There is a theory that the methane itself may be harming the ozone layer while destroying the excess oxygen. Whatever the causes there does not seem to be any very urgent measures being taken to prevent it happening apart from exhorting people not to use aerosols.

I suppose there would be a loss of profit until something else is discovered and accepted to take the place of the deadly chlorines.

What is human health (and animal health) compared to profits? Perhaps when it is no longer safe to lie in the Sun at all, the tourist industry might be able to persuade Governments of all the countries to do something about it. By that time of course it might be already too late.

There also seems to be more ozone at ground level, produced mainly by the combustion engines in cars, and this is poisonous to human and animal life.

> "I tell you naught for your comfort,
> Yea, nought for your desire,

Save that the sky grows darker yet,
and the sea rises higher."
G. K. Chesterton.

BOOKS WHICH DEAL MORE FULLY WITH THE SUBJECT

Secret life of plants, by Peter Tomkins and Christopher Bird.
The Deadly feast of life by Donald E. Carr.
Nature, Mother of invention, by Felix Paturi.
Extinction: the causes and consequences of the disappearance of species, by Paul and Anne Ehrlich.
The sex life of plants, by Alec Bristow.
Encyclopedia of the plant kingdom, edited by Anthony Huxley.
Nature magnified, by Lennart Nilsson.

CHAPTER II

YOU

You are unique. A one-off. Since mankind began there have never been two human beings exactly alike, not even identical twins (genetic engineers were trying to clone sheep when I wrote this so they may be cloning human babies by now, and they would certainly all be alike.)

You are the centre of your own universe. The only things you really know are the things you have actually experienced. Everything else is hearsay.

You do not know even if the colours you see are exactly the same colours that anyone else sees, if the smells you smell exactly match the smells that others smell, or even if the things you eat taste the same to others.

They are probably fairly near the same, but as we are all different so naturally our senses are different. No matter how many friends or relations you have in this world you are actually alone.

Nobody but you can know exactly how you feel, or what you are thinking, no matter how hard you try to explain. This goes for all the teeming millions of us. All alone in our heads.

We do most of our living in our heads. While busily (or idly) performing all sorts of actions and tasks, we usually find we are thinking of something quite different from what we are doing. It is usually only when something really interests us that we can become completely and utterly engrossed in whatever we are doing. We have no real control over our minds.

We all seem to need illusions about ourselves to help us to survive. I wonder if animals need such illusions? Someone once said that the message of Eugene O'Neill's play *The Iceman Cometh* was:

> "Truth is a form of aversion therapy alienating people from themselves. Take away anyone's pretentions and underneath there is nothing but anger, hatred, and a terrible feeling of inadequacy. Everybody needs their pipe-dreams, their lingering hopes and beliefs. We have to tell ourselves lies about ourselves to survive."

Is this true?

WHO ARE YOU?

We do not know ourselves. We cannot know ourselves. We do not even know how we will react to unusual circumstances until they actually happen, and then we are often surprised at our reactions.

I often wonder what people discover when they go away somewhere to "find themselves." Who is the "I" they are seeking. We cannot know. We all see ourselves as someone quite different from the person we appear to be to others. You may get a shock if you overhear someone describing you, or talking about you to another person. "Would some power, The giftie gie us, To see ourselves, as others see us," wrote Robert Burns about a cootie (louse) on a lady's hat in Church.

Everybody judges everybody else by their looks, their clothes, their mannerisms, their voices, their accents, the houses they inhabit, their cars and other status symbols, for their affluence, or lack of it. We all judge everyone in this way. You judge others and they judge you.

Others do not recognise the 'inner' person inside the body that they are looking at, any more than you recognise their true selves. This particularly applies to the old. Inside they still feel as young as they ever were. Only their bodies have aged. But we all behave towards them as if they were decrepit and not just their bodies.

We mostly approve of the rich, no matter how they've obtained their money. It still makes them powerful.

We approve of the beautiful. As in fairy stories the beautiful must have beautiful natures because they have beautiful faces and lovely bodies.

We approve of the famous, even if they are only famous for being famous like so-called television personalities.

We disapprove of the ugly, especially the old and ugly. They are always the villains in stories.

David Cecil once said:

> "Beautiful people are the blood royal of humanity, and are not governed by the same rules as ordinary mortals"

But very few people (except those who aspire to become President of the U.S.A. or other countries) are as confident of themselves as they lead other people to think they are. However, some are better at appearing confident. We judge everyone by their outward appearance and do not notice that they are bluffing.

Unpopular people are usually unpopular with everyone. That is their misfortune and there is usually nothing much they can do about it. You cannot change the nature you were born with.

You can, and usually do try to modify your behaviour to fit in with the people with whom you live and the society in which you live.

Those born with happy dispositions manage to be happy in the worst of environments and in the most adverse conditions. I do not mean that your environment has no effect on you. Far from it. If you are ill-fed, ill-used, ill-housed, and ill-treated you may have little hope of becoming the human being that life intended you to be. Your mind as well as your body will suffer from your deprivations. And suffering does not enoble the spirit. It gives you a feeling of resentment, 'a chip on your shoulder'; it enrages you against the world and everyone in it. Never suffer in silence. Relief, if there is any to be had, usually goes to those who make the most fuss, the ones with the loudest wails, the most demanding, the entirely self-centred. Of course, if you are good-looking, people will more readily come to your assistance. They may not bother if you are ill-favoured, deformed in mind or body, or old.

To be poor is the worst crime in this world. You are looked down upon by all. Everybody thinks they have the right to be patronising to you at the very least. But to be poor, disabled, ugly and old, is really to be at the bottom of the heap.

How do you secretly think about the poor? Do you think it is all their own fault?

Handsome people never seem to realise how much their good looks have eased their path through life until their looks desert them.

HOW DO WE TREAT THE NON-FAVOURED?

It is no longer popular to deride people's infirmities, so we tend to ignore the disabled in mind or body in the hope that they will go away and we can forget them. We used to put them into institutions so that we never needed to bother about them.

At one time in the past it was fashionable to visit asylums for the insane just to make fun of them. Now that they are supposed to be in the care of the Community they mostly seem to end up on the streets and nobody is looking after them. But the instinct to make fun or be violent towards the disabled or the different, is still there. People who wear glasses are still called "four-eyes" among other names which inhibits some youngsters (and oldsters) from wearing spectacles when they really need them.

As Dorothy Parker wrote: "Men seldom make passes at girls in glasses."

Ogden Nash replied: "But safety pins and bassinets* await the girl who fascinets"

Not everyone is able to wear contact lenses.

Women are not put off by men wearing glasses, but then women do not look at men in the same way that men look at women.

Children who have not been checked (or who are not under supervision) will jeer at, and imitate the crippled. They will not only call them names but they will physically attack them for not being what they consider normal. They will attack others for being of a different colour. They will attack others because they are weak or old and not able to defend themselves. Not all

---

*Bassinets used to be American for 'baby buggies'.

children behave like this, but a lot of youngsters become bullies against vulnerable people especially if the youngsters are in gangs. Mob rule takes over, and when they get older they carry on terrorising people if no-one stops them.

YOU ARE AN ACCIDENT

Blind chance is responsible for whichever genes you inherit from your parents. You may have been a 'planned' child in as much as your parents decided they wanted a child at that time, but nevertheless you are an accident, as we are all accidents. Nobody has any control over which genes are transmitted by which male sperm and female ovum.

Parents should not be disappointed with their children, and children should not be disappointed with their parents. Some often are. The difficult art (or craft) of being a parent is never appreciated by children until they become parents themselves.

At first, in the child's eyes, the parents are the world and know everything. By puberty, the parents are old-fashioned and know nothing.

The wealthy in this country have mainly avoided the perils of parentage by having their young brought up first by nursemaids and nannies and then sending their young (especially the boys) to institutions called Preparatory schools and later private schools called Public schools. So they need see very little of their children except during the school holidays.

By which ever method the children are brought up, it is the wrong method in the child's eyes and the children are determined to bring up their own children in a different manner (except for those who were sent to boarding schools and hated it and who nevertheless send their young sons to the same places. Why?) Thus everything goes from laxity to severity and back again with each generation having its own ideas on what is important in bringing up children.

But very few parents seem to look back to their own childhood and remember what it was like to be a child, and apply those memories to their own children.

Nearly all children think their parents got it wrong and that their children are having a better time than they did. A perpetual illusion?

There is a theory that every child is the offspring of his maternal grandmother and his father. The theory says that a woman's ovaries and potential eggs (ova) are present when she is born so they must have been produced by her mother. A man's sperm is newly made; so that a pregnancy in a twenty year old woman means that a twenty year old egg is impregnated with the newly made sperm!

Thus it is that the continuity of the human (and animal race) is always through the female line. The males supply the variations and the males.

YOUR BODY

You have very little control over the workings of your body. LIFE has taken over the highly organised factory that is your body and LIFE, not you, is in charge.

If you are in perfect health you do not even notice your body unless it is touching something. There is feeling of nothingness. You do not even notice how your body is behaving until something is wrong. You may be completely unaware of it until you get a pain somewhere, which may be a signal to you to stop whatever you are doing to injure your body.

You may be giving it unsuitable food, or drink or medicants or drugs. Or even working it too hard. Or it is maybe having difficulty combatting some of the millions of germs with which we are all surrounded.

We are all hosts to millions of mites and bacteria. Some are in the follicles of our skin. Surgeons are now finding that "scrubbing up" before an operation disturbs millions of these bacteria, and brings them to the surface of the skin. We also have millions of bacteria in our mouths and in our digestive systems. We could not function without them. They all prevent our bodies from breaking down. So, when LIFE leaves us, it also leaves the millions of microbes to whom, we are, each of us, a world.

Read the little book *"The life that lives on man"* by Michael Andrews, if you can bear it.

LIFE knows better than your conscious mind what your body needs. If your body indicates that it wants a rest, give it a rest; do not try to pep it up. We should all learn as much as we can about the workings of our bodies. Many a man knows a lot more about how his car works than how his body works. Knowing something of your body's workings might make you less neurotic or less of a hyperchondriac than if you know nothing. You also might be better able to tell your doctor when something is wrong just where the trouble is. Many of us see a doctor for five minutes or less and have to accept his snap judgement. Furthermore, nobody ever wants to know the side effects of any nostrum he prescribes. Most people hesitate to antagonise their doctor by telling him that his medicines have ill effects, so they just throw his medicines away after giving them a trial.

If patients were given pre-paid forms with any new medicine, that they could send to some central agency with a computer, when they had any side effects from the said medicine, the side effects could become known before much damage was done.

Women should learn as much as possible about their reproductive systems. Doctors often disagree with this saying that unsterilised instruments could be used. One woman on a T.V. programme about this subject said "Nobody suggests boiling a penis for ten minutes before inserting it in a vagina."

Cancer of the cervix is a disease of women caused, it is thought, by sexual intercourse (not necessarily caused by intercourse with more than one man.) Nuns never get it, and I am told that fewer Jewish women get it than non-Jewish women. This may be because male Jews are circumcised as babies thus having the foreskin of the penis removed. It has been said that some men do not wash under the foreskin as they should, so that those in jobs where cancer-causing dust and chemicals are used, are in danger of giving their partners cancer.

YOUR MIND

Who said: "Do not adjust your mind, there is fault in reality."?

Most people agree that your mind is somewhere in your brain. But where? Nobody knows. In fact we know very little about the brain and the way it works. Of course there are theories.

We give depressed people electric shock treatment, which is said to relieve their depression in some cases. Nobody knows why giving somebody what looks like an epileptic fit can relieve anything.

There are theories about which part of the brain does what, and which bit is the language centre that all mankind possesses and other animals seem to lack. But where is the memory located?

Mental health as well as physical health depends on what you eat. It was well said "A healthy mind in a healthy body"

Allergies to various foods can make people behave in abnormal ways. Wheat is a culprit not often suspected. Artificial colouring in foods can trigger odd behaviour. Children and adults can have iron deficiency anaemia, which can also lead to disruptive behaviour, as can vitamin deficiencies.

Now that the Government has authorised the irradiation of fruit and vegetables merely to prolong their shelf life, more people will suffer from a lack of vitamin C as it is mostly removed by this process.

Lead is a toxic metal that is thought, like cadmium to affect the brain.

Some motorists now use lead-free petrol but not yet enough of them yet to notice any improvement in the behaviour and mental alertness of children said to be suffering from lead poisoning.

We mostly buy our food from supermarkets, these days. Food already prepared and overwrapped. Some of it just junk food. Women cook a lot less than they used to do. Buying something to heat up in the microwave is easier when you are short of time because you have a job outside the home. Nobody can tell what the effect of this sort of food will have on future generations.

If you are a prospective mother your diet is doubly important if you want a healthy child, and to avoid the risk of having a miscarriage or a child with *spina bifida* (an incompletely formed brain and spinal column), you should eat foods rich in vitamins such as lettuce, fruit, nuts and lightly cooked green vegetables such as peas and beans (frozen if no fresh is available) broccoli, cabbage and sprouts and also brown rice and bread. Vitamin B is easily destroyed by heat, light and lengthy storage so it is safe to take vitamin B tablets as well. They do not have any side effects. You cannot know which foods have been irradiated with loss of vitamins, and now that the Foodco of San Diego California believes it can increase the shelf-life of dairy products and fruit juices and egg mixes without spoiling the flavour, but with no mention of loss of nutrition, or vitamins, but subjecting the food to pulses of a high electric field while heating it to around 50c or so, once again we shall have to be very careful of what we eat. What happens in America today happens here tomorrow.

It is also wise to take vitamin C and E tablets and zinc. Other birth defects such as diabetes, Down's syndrome and epilepsy seem to be caused by genetic changes in parental germ cells in both men's sperm and women's eggs. These changes could be caused by alcohol, cannabis, tobacco, diesel engine fumes, overheated cooking oil, coal dust, radiation and various drugs including valium and paracetamol. Avoid as many as you can. It is a wonder than anyone is born without defects!

Also women should have their thyroid glands checked. Apparently a lack of iodine can cause brain damage in babies. In women genetic mutations seem to take place three days before ovulation and ends the day after conception. In men it can begin as early as four months before conception. In hospitals in Stockholm investigations in miscarriages found that about half were attributed to abnormal sperm in the men caused by the same genetic changes as in the woman. Sometimes repeated miscarriages can be caused by the woman drinking too much coffee or even by a slight zinc deficiency in the man. Of course excessive lead or excessive pesticide residues in the body (from all the pesticides sprayed over many of the things we eat) can also cause damaged babies or miscarriages.

Fish can be contaminated by sewage, heavy metals and chemical spills etc. Apples were sprayed with Alar. Has that yet been stopped? Can we be sure that red meat is entirely free from B.S.E. (*bovine spongiform encephalopathy*) otherwise "mad cow disease"?

Spraying of pesticides in rural areas leads to asthma and allergies in children exposed to spray drift and residues. There is no legal obligation for farmers to notify anyone in the vicinity about spraying.

CONSTIPATION

Constipation, judging by all the laxatives advertised, is a problem for many people.

Constipation is usually a result of a poor diet lacking in sufficient roughage, or as it is called these days, fibre. Of course we nearly all suffer from constipation from the first day we go to school. We were all told, "Wait until break", which was decidedly not what our bodies wanted.

Then we were given laxatives to counteract the constipation and thus our bodies got into habits whereby we were unable to function without the laxatives, thus enriching the manufacturers of pharmaceutical concoctions.

Nobody knows the ultimate result of this self-poisoning.

It is becoming more difficult to know what to eat without

being made ill. We have had "mad cow" disease which has put us off red meat. We have *salmonella* which puts us off eggs. We have had *listeria* in soft cheeses. Apples have been sprayed with a poison that does not wash off. Potatoes are sprayed with a chemical which prevents them from sprouting. And we know that farm crops are sprayed many times before they are harvested. Farm animals are treated with anti-biotics to prevent the spread of disease in the inhumane manner in which most of them live out their short lives.

On T.V. in a children's programme about animals we were told that bats were dying out, despite being covered by a preservation order, because they used to live on insects found in cow pats, but now because of the anti-biotics given to the cows their cow pats are completely sterile.

All other carnivorous animals, insects and birds eat their prey alive, or freshly killed, except man and the carrion crows, vultures etc. Man is the only creature that cooks flesh before eating it, and sometimes chooses to cook it many days after it has been killed, and sometimes even when it is going rotten.

When and how did man learn to cook? Was it a form of preservation for when he could not hunt? Man is the only animal to cook other animals when they are still alive. We boil lobsters alive. They turn from blue to red. Do they scream? We boil crayfish and shrimps alive. The Japanese and the French (perhaps others) fry fish alive. Do these cooks deserve the same treatment?

KNOWLEDGE OF PLANTS THAT ARE GOOD TO EAT

In the Western world we seem to have lost our instinctive

knowledge of plants that are good to eat. There must be thousands of plants we could make use of out of the 300,000 reputed species in the world. We do use more than we used to do since we have discovered Indian and Chinese cookery, even if we only use the supermarket versions.

There is a movement to get us to use more organically grown food, that is food grown without the use of pesticides and other poisons, but because there is at present so little call for it, it is much more expensive and difficult to come by.

Wild animals seem to know which plants are good for them. Of course those who eat the widest range of plants are the ones most likely to survive. Those who live on one plant only can be wiped out if the plant fails. One example is the Giant Panda of China which is supposed to live entirely on bamboo shoots.

Many wild pandas were found dead in China because the bamboo crop had failed. As they are one of the endangered species of animals they may soon become extinct. Many Zoos have failed to get them to breed, but a Zoo in Mexico is reported to have bred them and fed them on other things than bamboo shoots.

MILLIONS OF PEOPLE STILL STARVE

Henry Cantwell Wallace once said: "Nations can only endure as long as their topsoil."

Although a lot more of the world is turning into desert probably because of overuse of the soil, this statement may not be true for ever as scientists are learning to grow yeasts and bacteria for animal food (and maybe human food?) on oil and various industrial wastes. In fact there are some who think that we should not waste fossil fuel on burning it for heating, or to run cars, when it could be more usefully used.

There is no need for millions of people to starve if food was given top priority instead of every nation wasting its resources on buying armaments and waging war.

There is most probably enough food already produced in the world to feed everyone, but there is, as yet, no agreement on the ways in which this food could be distributed. People will only produce and sell for profit.

Some of the poorer countries do not wish to accept the charity of the richer nations (except in times of famine) especially if the charity has strings attached, as it usually has. They wish to retain their own independence. And human nature being what it is, even if the food is accepted, there are as many corrupt people in the poorer countries as there are in the richer, so free food rarely reaches the ones it is intended to feed.

SLEEP

We all need sleep. But why should we? Nobody knows. We say we sleep because we are tired. But just resting should be the answer to that.

The factory that we call our body does not shut down during sleep. Our hearts, lungs, digestion etc. go on functioning but maybe at a slower rate.

Our brains certainly do not shut down. We dream and apparently it is essential that we dream. People in laboratory experiments have been awakened every time their rapid eye movements during sleep have indicated that they were dreaming. After a few nights of this prevention of dreaming, their behaviour deteriorates, they hallucinate, and become fretful and sometimes quite violent. But what are our brains and minds doing during this dreaming? Nobody really knows, but many theories abound. The only dreams that we remember are the ones in which we wake up while still dreaming, and we only remember them usually for a very short time, unless we make a very real effort to recall them. Nightmares are easier to remember because of the terror involved. Some dreams are so vivid that it is sometimes difficult to decide, when we wake, which is the dream and which is the reality. Some dreams have a tenuous connection with the events of the previous day, especially anxiety dreams. Some have a physical cause, like dreaming you are climbing a mountain and awaking to find you have backache. Animals dream as you can see if you watch your cats' or dog's legs twitching and running as they sleep.

People who can cat-nap and who can fall asleep as soon as they lie down, do not realise how lucky they are compared with those who have great difficulty in getting to sleep. Insomniacs need just as many hours of sleep so they waste a lot of their time in fruitless efforts to go to sleep, and then get up late, or feel tired all day because they did not get their full sleep quota. It is mostly the lucky sleepers who write books on how to relax and go to sleep, for the rest of us poor mortals. They have usually experienced a short time during an illness when they have lost their normal ease of getting to sleep. They imagine when this ease returns that they have caused it to return by some relaxing routine, and they wish to tell the rest of the world how to do it. Alas, it never works for near insomniacs. Not even hypnotism will help, because only those who fall asleep easily are easy to hypnotise. Some lucky folks need very little sleep. Think how much more pleasure they can get from all those extra hours.

There are others who say they never sleep.

Some food researchers suggest that a meal high in carbohydrates just before bed might help some to sleep. It may increase the amount of serotonin in the brain which is thought to be the key to sleep. Scientists working for drug companies searching for the perfect sleeping pill call the substance 'Factor S' and hope to retrieve enough from animal brains from slaughter houses to analyse it and then synthenise it. Or am I already out-of-date? I have not yet heard of the perfect sleeping pill, only of more so-called safe pills that have turned out to have unpleasant side effects.

NUDITY

Why is there a continual prurient curiosity about nakedness? We all have the same sort of bodies. Man is just a naked ape according to Desmond Morris. Most other creatures have fur, feathers, scales etc. (except worms and new-born birds etc.) but even if they were naked they would not presumably be interested as long as the males can find the females and the females can find the males. Perhaps we all should spend some time at a "nude" beach (in the sun) or join a nudist society. Are we all ashamed of our bodies? Primitive peoples seem to have had no hang-ups about being naked. It cannot all stem from the fig-leaf episode in the garden of Eden, in the Bible.

ENERGY

Some lucky people have enormous amounts of energy and

regard those who are not so fortunate as lazy, when they really should be commiserating with them as everything to them is an up-hill struggle.

HAPPINESS

Happiness is defined in one dictionary as a state of "being joyful, contented, cheerful, pleased with life, pleased with success, good fortune and participation in what is considered good and kind; well adapted to a purpose, suitable, apt; bringing about or indicating joy and delight." This is a good try, but happiness is really indefinable. We are (most of us) in search of it, but even if we find it we can only sustain it for short periods. We can settle for contentment and cheerfulness for longer periods, but, human nature being what it is, boredom sets in and we crave excitement even at the expense of contentment. Pleasure in success and good fortune is often fleeting so happiness can still elude us. Happiness for some can only be seen in retrospect (probably through rose-coloured spectacles). They say "We were happy then" but at that time they would never have admitted to being happy. Happiness seems to be an elusive goal, a will-o-the-wisp but we all catch sight of it at some time in our lives. Perhaps the lower your expectations are, the more likely you are to experience it, sometimes in moments that would seem like nothing to those in more fortunate circumstances.

Maybe our impoverished ancestors would have thought that happiness included a comfortable bed, free from fleas and bugs, a centrally heated house (unheard of since Roman times, and then only for the rich) a radio, and especially television, (if they could have imagined such a thing) more leisure, and a car instead of a horse for transport.

Most of us have all these things, but we find that possessions do not bring lasting happiness (except for the young on their birthdays and at Christmas if they have been given what they were longing for.) Who said: "I believe that happiness is the only good; the place to be happy is here; and the time to be happy is now."?

A SOUL?

Most of mankind seems to think it has a soul, or an inner spirit. Most religions include a soul for man. But what is it? This belief may have come from those who claim to have had astral projections, that is, they feel that they have another spiritual body which can rise above to observe their actual body usually when lying in bed. This happens during sleep or unconsciousness, but is afterwards remembered.

Doctors and others were sceptical about these happenings until some patients who had died for a little while, perhaps only seconds, were resuscitated and described how they hovered above themselves and watched all the resuscitation processes. These descriptions have, so I am told, been accurate even when the processes used were so new or different from the usual processes that the patient could not otherwise have known about them.

This is raising questions of whether we have yet another state of consciousness. It may happen to everybody at the time of their death but we shall never know. This astral projection may also explain why some folk have claimed to see events that have happened at some distance from them.

"There are more things in Heaven and Earth, Horatio,
Than are dreamt of in your philosophy."
"Hamlet" Shakespeare

CHAPTER III

MEN AND WOMEN

ARE MEN SUPERFLUOUS?

Ever since man started domesticating animals as food stocks, many thousands, maybe millions of years ago, he has realised that most males are superfluous.

A farmer used to keep one good bull for his herd of cows, and castrated all the other males; one good ram for his flock of sheep; and if he kept horses he sent his mares to a good stallion and castrated his other stallions. Now of course he probably relies on artificial insemination or buys embryos, and keeps no males at all. All he needs for food and profit are females to breed from and he slaughters any males when young, or castrates them. So is this one of the reasons why men, in the main, hate women and ignore their very existence (except for nubile young women, and their own families, or any woman they fancy as a sexual partner) Are they afraid that women will one day decide that they can do without men?

WOMEN REALLY LIKE MEN

They need have no fear. LIFE has so ordained it that women actually like men. In fact they idolise them (or most of them) no matter how badly they behave. LIFE has made women inordinately fond of their sons (there are of course a few exceptions)

Some mothers are even willing to sacrifice the lives of their daughters if they think their sons are in need. If you remember the film *Sophie's Choice* the choice was which of her children should go to the gas chambers to save the life of the other one. She chose to send her daughter to save the life of her son. Most mothers would have done the same.

When food is scarce in poorer countries, what food there is, is given to the boys' and the girls are left to starve. I remember an Englishwoman telling me about her sister and her sister's children. She said: "She loves the girls but she would still make them into soup if the boy needed it." Thus, are the human males preserved.

Nature (LIFE) makes some women treat their sons as Gods and their daughters as lesser mortals. Of course most mothers deny this, and tell you they treat all their children alike, but, if you listen to them talking to the boys who can usually get away with any sort of behaviour, and then listen to them talking to their girls, whose behaviour is very strictly restrained, you will realise that they do not even notice what they are doing. Because the daughters are female and the mothers are female the mothers think they understand their daughters, but because they do not understand their sons they somehow think that they are simpler to understand. Some of them are just simply overcome by producing male children.

In this man's world, men are constantly denigrating women and trying to make them look ridiculous even in their own eyes. If any woman objects she is told they are only teasing "and can't you take a joke." It is no joke. It is nothing but sheer spite in most cases. Men like nubile girls as sexual objects (next to money, cars and sport, some men seem to think of nothing else. Life seems to have programmed them to think of sex every five minutes) They tolerate women (their wives or others) who will do their household chores or any job they dislike doing.

As an example of men's attitude to women, I remember a fairly well-known T.V. interviewer talking to a young woman who expected her husband to share the housework because she worked as many hours at her job as he did at his. The interviewer asked in horrified tones "You surely would not expect you husband to scrub the floors?" the girl answered "Why not if they needed scrubbing?" Whereupon the interviewer asked her if she was not in danger of losing her femininity. I never understood before what femininity meant. Now I know it means being a general dogsbody, and doing all the menial tasks that are beneath a man's dignity to perform, at least in the home.

Most men do not like women as people. Of course there are many men who love their wives, but even they rarely regard them as people to be listened to, and not just to be talked at.

WOMEN IN PARLIAMENT

We know that there are very few women in Parliament and that there should really be many more.

A Conservative M.P. Theresa Gorman said that male M.P's aloof indifference to women's topics has shocked her. She tried to get a private member's bill passed proposing that each constituency should be represented by one man and one woman. Of course it met with hoots of derision from all the male M.P's. Naturally half the men would lose their seats.

This is not a new idea. G.B. Shaw proposed it half a century ago, in a famous letter to Lady Rhondda of 'Time and Tide'. But it is the only way forward for women, plus half the Cabinet being women, and women not like Mrs Thatcher who always thinks like a man and did nothing to improve anything for women during her long reign as Prime Minister.

Men will not give up their power willingly, so women will have to fight for this just as the Suffragettes fought for the vote. This means that women will have to support women which many today do not do, having been brought up to think that men are superior instead of the six-year olds that most of them are.

JOKES ABOUT WOMEN

Many so-called comedians are always making disparaging remarks and so-called jokes about their (pretend) wives and mothers-in-law.

Why do women laugh with the men at these put-downs? The women cannot think that belittling remarks about themselves are funny. I think they mostly pretend to think they are funny to please the men.

Women comedians do not make the same sort of belittling remarks about their (pretend) husbands because they know the men would regard them as the insults they are, and as the employers are men they would soon be out of a job.

Most mothers-in-law treat their sons-in-law much better than they deserve. It is the wives who often have cause to complain. A lot of mothers think that no girl is good enough for her precious son, whom she has brought up to expect the same sort of complete devotion to his every need, from his wife, as his mother has given him. And naturally she is jealous because he prefers another woman to her, which is understandable.

Women often do not behave naturally with men other than

their immediate family. They can behave naturally with other women when there are no men present. With men they play-act and aim to please even when they have no sexual intentions. They just pander to the men. Is this inborn, or is it due to being brought up in a male dominated society? Seeing baby girls flirting with their fathers makes me wonder.

WOMEN AS PROPERTY

The denigrating of women by men goes back a long way in history, probably because being bigger and stronger (men seldom realise how much stronger they are) brings out the bully in many people, just as it does in animals, and gives them the urge to dominate, and exact obedience. It is not so long ago that even in this country men were allowed by law to beat their wives. Although the law has been changed the beatings still go on. A punch in the face has been many a husband's answer to any argument with his wife.

Women were, and still are, in some parts of the world, regarded as property to be disposed of just as the father or even brother wishes.

Many a play or opera plot hinges on the reluctance of the daughter to marry the man her father has given or more likely sold her to. I cite *Romeo and Juliet* and *A Midsummer's Night's Dream* as examples.

Juliet was her father's property to bestow as he pleased, and she had no say in who she was to marry; hence the tragedy. Many girls were married off to neighbouring landowners to increase the family's holdings. The girl had no choice even if the prospective bridegroom was old enough to be her grandfather.

In some countries the girls are still sold by their fathers to which ever prospective husband will pay the highest bride price. If the prospective husband dies, she then becomes the property of the next eldest brother, even if that brother is only a schoolboy. The girl then joins her new family as partial slave to her mother-in-law.

Women are often jealous of younger women (as are men of younger men) so will meet out to her young daughter-in-law the same treatment that they themselves received in a spirit of 'why should she have a better time than I did'.

In other societies a father has to provide a dowry for his daughter as a gift to his son-in-law or the man's family. When the families in days gone by (we hope) were too poor to afford dowries they would kill off the new-born girls.

This still goes on (the dowry system) in India and there have been numerous reports of bride-burning because the dowry was not considered sufficient or the promised motor-cycle and television set did not arrive. The women paid with their lives. This burning of brides is reported to be happening in the U.K. where the dowries were not as promised. Sometimes they were reported as kitchen accidents but everybody knew what had really happened.

Of course India has a tradition of death by burning for unwanted women. It is reported that widows are still being burnt alive on their husbands funeral pyres and people in India think it is admirable. This practice was called *suttee* and was supposed to have been stopped during British rule in India. But it seems to be happening all over again with widows throwing themselves on the burning pyres because they have been left destitute. Other widows if younger can only escape starvation by becoming prostitutes.

INFANTICIDE

The Chinese used to expose their unwanted girl babies for the wild beasts to kill and eat. Perhaps it was because the ones who were Buddhists would not do their own killing. (Buddhists have often employed mercenaries to do their killing for them in war; I cannot see that it is any different from doing your own killing.)

An Indian caste of priests were known as the daughter-killers because they only ever allowed the boys to live. The boys were married off to the girls of wealthy families of an equal caste.

In the Western world, including the United Kingdom, infanticide appears to have been fairly common until contraceptives became available. Of course many young children died of diseases that today can be cured. Nobody has ever enquired about the feelings of the mothers of these discarded children.

THE BASIC SEX

Why did men invent the Biblical myth that woman was formed from a man's rib? Was this just jealousy because they knew that all life springs from the female? Is this the way men have tried to prove their superiority when they knew they were not the basic sex?

All life continues through the females. The males provide the males and the variations. We now know that we inherit what have been named chromosomes from our mothers and fathers (men through the ages have pretended to think that men provided the seed and women only provided the womb in which their seed grew). We inherit X chromosomes from the mother and either an X or Y chromosome from the father.

X chromosomes from both parents results in a girl, and a Y chromosome from the father results in a boy.

Women have been blamed for centuries because they gave birth to girls when their husbands wanted boys, but it has only been discovered fairly recently that the sex of the child is determined by the man's chromosome, and the man's alone.

Strangely the number of females and males born in any community (where the females are not discarded) seems to be fairly even. However, the balance of the sexes could drastically alter in the future when everyone will be able to decide on the sex of their children.

In China in an effort to restrict population (already one fourth of the world's population) the people are being told to have only one child. It is still a Communist country so personal liberty is restricted. Laws have had to be passed to try to prevent fathers from murdering their child if it is a girl, because they all want boys to carry on the family name, and help with the farm, and presumably to look after them in their old age.

I do not know if there are old-age pensions provided in China, but I do know that any family restrictions in any country will not work unless parents can be assured of some means of support when they get too old or too infirm to support themselves.

MEN'S VIRILITY

To many men their sex and virility are the most important aspects of their lives. But, because LIFE has been so stingy in making mankind's (and animals') excretory organs serve a double purpose, men and women, (as far as we know) have always been ashamed of their origins (perhaps not in India judging by their

Temple pictures and sculptures). This shame is what makes it difficult for parents to tell their children about sex. This shame makes men think that women are debased by allowing men to have sexual intercourse with them especially if the women enjoy it. As a young boy, before he knows what are euphemistically called "the facts of life" he cannot imagine his mother letting his father do this to her, and if he is told "the facts of life" he will not believe it. If he is told in lessons at school he is more inclined to believe it.

When a boy reaches puberty it results in him having a different attitude to his mother, but still, when his friends are making their usual lewd remarks about girls and women he will get annoyed if they make them about his mother, his sisters, his wife, or his daughters. Any other female is fair game.

HOMOSEXUALITY

Sometimes if a boy's love for his mother remains excessive it may be difficult for him to think of having sex with a woman and although he may not be genetically homosexual it may push him in that direction. As the graffiti has it:

"My mother made me a homosexual."

Somebody wrote underneath

"If I sent her the wool would she make me one?"

Heterosexual men and boys learn to be homosexuals when they are herded together without girls and women, as in boarding schools, the Armed forces, and of course prisons.

Bisexuality has gone on through the ages. We are told that the ancient Greeks (with their much-vaunted civilisation) had their boys as a matter of course.

The ancient Chinese are supposed to have had a saying "A woman for duty, a boy for pleasure, and a goat for ecstasy." Whether this is a Western libel I do not know.

Genetically homosexual men (presumably the feminine ones) have a distinctive sort of voice and manner that proclaims them for all the world to know. They are not believable if they try to pretend otherwise.

HERMAPHRODITES

Women would have been happier if LIFE had not made two sexes but just one, hermaphrodites, two sexes in one, where they all had the young, and no one sex could be dominant.

Only pretty young girls can think otherwise just as long as they can twist any man round their little finger, but as they get older they will realise they no longer have that power.

There was a programme on T.V. called 'Nature Watch' in which an Australian housewife, named I think, Densy Cline, showed photographs she had taken of tiger slugs (striped) coiled in exotic spirals, dangling from threads spun by each, while white sex organs came out of their heads, and being hermaphrodites they impregnated each other. It seems a shame that LIFE did not take the same sort of path like this for mankind. White sex organs emanating from the head could never have been thought shameful.

Men and women would all have had the same life experience and all could understand one another much better that most men and women understand one another now. But men will say *"Vive la difference"*. But think how much better life would have been for many women even now. And if you have noticed homosexuals can fall in love with one another just as passionately as heterosexuals fall in love with one another, and more often can become close friends than can many a married couple, just because they have had the same life and biological experience. I have also noticed how homosexuals tend to get on very well conversationally with women because they pose no sort of threat and need no play-acting.

In one part of the world (I forget where) the women had been feeding the chickens on birth control pills because the oestrogen made them grow bigger, and some of the boys, when fed on the chickens, became hermaphrodites. When offered an operation they all decided to become men not women. They realised that men can have a more interesting and freer life than women. They are more likely to be able to take care of themselves when violence erupts.

They are free to go anywhere in the world without being molested. They do not have to be afraid to go out in the dark. There are many more professions and jobs open to them and they get more money for doing these jobs, so they are financially independent, as most women are not. And there are always women to take care of them and wait on them.

As most men have sex on the brain (by LIFE'S design) they can get some pleasure out of seeing all the young nubile women even to the age when they are no longer capable of being sexually active. And they do not have to bear the children.

BACHELORS AND SPINSTERS

Bachelors (male) always seem to be respected, but the woman who does not marry or live with a man (unless of course she has become a nun,) is called various uncomplimentary names and often despised by other women because she did not "get her man" even if she did not want any of them. As Jane Austen says in *Emma* Chapter 10.

> "A single woman with a very narrow income must be a ridiculous, disagreeable old maid; the proper sport of boys and girls; but a single woman of good fortune is always respectable, and may be as sensible and pleasant as anybody else. It is only poverty which makes a woman's celibacy contemptible to the general public"

The woman who lets many men have sex with her is called by men a slut, a slag or any other contemptible name they can think of, and is despised by both men and women. The woman who needs sex nearly as much as the average man is called a nymphomaniac or worse.

The man who has sex with many women boasts of his conquests to other men and is regarded with admiration by them (as long as his conquests are not their women) He is "a bit of a lad" or whatever the current phrase is. Men who so use women are known as womanisers and are esteemed by their fellow men. "A man who strays is a bit of a dog, but a woman who strays is a complete bitch."

This double standard seems to have existed all through recorded history. Of course very few men would want to raise another man's bastard child.

In Victorian times or even Edwardian, respectable women were supposed to have no sexual feelings and just put up with their husband's demands for sex just to indulge them.

As sex never seems to have been mentioned in mixed company and certainly never discussed, the women probably had very little to enjoy, their husband's love-making (so-called) being often aggressive and akin to rape with no thought but for their own pleasure.

I think it was a bit of a shock to many soldiers when they went to India and found books and manuals such as the *Karma Sutra* which deal with the topic of love-making in an explicit manner.

Other soldiers found out that in Africa and some other countries terrible things were done to the women. They were sexually mutilated so that they could have no pleasure in sexual intercourse.

For some women, still, sex as indulged in by men is a form of hatred against women, but why men should hate women when a woman gave them life, I shall never know. In her book *The Female Eunuch* Germaine Greer remarked that women failed to understand just how much men hated them.

RAPE

Rape is a foul crime against women that still very rarely incurs the punishment that it deserves. It is often not reported to the police because of their still hostile attitude to the woman reporting it, although things are supposed to have improved. If a case gets to court the woman is treated as if she is the guilty party and the rape was all her own fault. Even when rapists threaten with knives judges still seem to think the woman could have prevented the rape. How? By being murdered? Even when men rape little girls judges have been known to call it a misdemeaner.

I suppose once again it is hatred for women that make men rape them to debase and humiliate them, perhaps because their mothers did not make enough fuss of them when they were young (or so the theory goes) So, when they rape old women of eighty-odd it must be because their grandmothers scorned them?

The accused, as in all criminal cases must seek to rebut a charge which imperils his liberty, but the prosecution witness is also at risk for if the jury do not believe her she is branded a liar.

The Law Lords ruled that a man cannot be guilty of rape if he honestly believed the woman consented and that is a defence put forward by all accused men.

There should be a law that the evidence of a woman's previous sexual history ought no longer to be admissible (except in cases where she has accused others of rape and jury has not believed her). Then the accused would be on trial and not the accuser as at present.

Women are told they are putting themselves at risk if they go out after dark, hitchhike, travel in an otherwise empty railway carriage etc. but why are women expected to trade in their freedom in order to be protected from violence?

Rape is humiliation and degradation.

In Iran a woman has to provide four male witnesses if she accuses a man of rape!

INCEST

Incest is usually between father and daughter, sometimes starting when the girl is only a baby. When the incest is committed by the father the girl is in a cleft stick. If she tells her mother she is likely to be sent away from home (often into care or an institution) to be well away from her father. If she tells anyone else, the father could go to prison and the whole family would suffer, being deprived of the breadwinner, and of course being shunned by everyone. Either way she is doubly the victim; she is the one who is punished for somebody else's crime.

If the incest is by an elder brother, her mother is not likely to believe her. If it is an uncle or close family friend she may be too frightened to tell her parents. Incest happens more often than most people can believe, and it is mostly undetected. Like rape, it can poison a girl's life.

PROSTITUTION

Prostitution either female or male would not exist unless there was a demand for it. It is known as the oldest profession in the world, so men must always have regarded the kept woman they married, as of a different sort from the often despised women they paid to have sex with, and often very peculiar forms of sex.

Women can be prosecuted for soliciting, but until now, and only in certain parts of the country can men, kerb-crawling in cars and soliciting any passing girl, be prosecuted. Men may be prosecuted for soliciting boys in public lavatories.

If a woman has other prostitutes in her house and sex is indulged in with customers (knows as punters) her house is classed as a brothel and can be shut down, and she and the other prostitutes sent to jail. But the punters are never named or prosecuted; without the customers there would be no prostitutes or brothels.

When the punters come from the most respected and richest

families in the land, the prostitutes can never name names because they know that if they do some terrible accident can befall them.

If the prostitutes have to rent rooms they are usually ripped off by the landlords or hotel-keepers. Most prostitutes have a man friend, presumably to protect them from the more violent of the clients, or to stop other men from preventing them from getting a living. Of course many of these men friends are the very ones that have made the girls go on the streets as prostitutes in the first place. The said ponce, or male friend can be prosecuted for living on immoral earnings if the prostitute is prosecuted. The strange thing is, the man is given a longer sentence, his being the worse offence, but because the men's prisons are full to bursting point (including prisoners on remand) he gets a suspended sentence, a pat on the wrist, while the female with a shorter sentence has to serve her sentence in prison just because women are more law-abiding and women's prisons are not full up.

Most of the inhabitants of women's prisons (apart from the habitual shop-lifters) should be in some sort of rehabilitation centre and not in prison at all. They are often mentally inadequate and often illiterate. They are always poor. The rich rarely land in jail (and if they do they get sent to open prisons and are released long before their sentence is up on some pretext or other) Like the men they can afford clever lawyers and belong to the same class as the judiciary, or what they may consider a higher class.

Why do women take up prostitution? In some cases they are pushed into it by their male friends. In others they think that with all the risks of getting A.I.D.S. and V.D. and hepatitis B. and meeting with violence, it is often more profitable than a life of domestic service, or working for poor wages in a factory for less money than the men doing the same job, or even poorer wages working at home doing sewing or small assembly jobs. Some women still work at home for a few pence an hour.

Most prostitutes seem to despise men, except for the ones who might make them rich and independent.

This is one of the few jobs where a woman with no qualifications and no money (to start with) if she is slightly attractive, can please herself when and where she works, that is, if she does not have a ponce forever wanting more money. It seems a very poor way of spending one's life but it is at least preferable to making bombs or armaments, or making war on people or animals.

I still think that prostitution should be legalised and the girls all in a red light district. Other women would not be harassed by curb-crawlers. The girls could have their own places and would not need ponces, and would not get ripped off for rent. They could all be medically examined so there might be less spread of sexual diseases. And there would be one less job for the police to do so that they could devote the time to preventing crime, and the magistrates courts would be less full. Legalised red light districts seem to work in other countries so I see no reason why they should not work here. It would save a lot of hypocrisy. Prostitution is never going to go away so it may as well be put on a legal basis (without any extra bureaucracy). I am not suggesting brothels owned and run by men. The law classes any house in which more than one woman engages in prostitution as a brothel, so let it be just that. Brothels without men owners or presiding "Madams", just two or three women living in the same house with the Council or Government or whoever ensuring that they are not ripped off when renting or buying a property and police protection like everyone else against violent clients or muggers or pimps and ponces.

There are now in all the larger cities, young boys and older boys acting as prostitutes to older men. They hang about anywhere where there is a so-called circus or roundabout where the punters can circle with their cars. The younger the boys are, the more money they can get, with twelve and thirteen year olds doing best. They are not called prostitutes, they are rent boys.

There was a T.V. programme about this newish problem which was only generally known about in Piccadilly Circus in London. I think the programme was probably a mistake as it suggested to a lot more youngsters that they too could cash in. They said the punters came from all walks of life, some of them being magistrates who even sentenced rent-boys brought before them, while they themselves were using rent-boys when out of the courts.

The rent-boys do not seem to be preyed on by ponces as do the female prostitutes. They do not rent rooms so there is no rip-off. Some do dress in drag so that the police will think they are women and will not stop the cars.

In 1992 in Birmingham the police decided to arrest the rent boys in the same way that they arrested women prostitutes but with the idea of rehabilitating them, not punishing them as they do the women. Of course the punters were not arrested.

MALE BEHAVIOUR

In primitive societies the women are usually expected to grow the crops, fetch the water (sometimes from miles away) find the fuel (sticks etc.) pound the crops to make bread, spin the wool and make the cloth and bring up the children etc. etc. The men often lead an idle life except when hunting or taking part in their games of dressing up and dancing and having ceremonies from which the women are excluded. And of course they make war on neighbouring tribes and carry off their women. This male behaviour occurs in the same sort of way in more civilised societies except that if there is any money to be made from any of the jobs, such as growing the crops, the men will take these jobs for themselves. The women can keep all the jobs that do not show a profit. Men have never liked women to have any financial independence.

Man is the only animal who demands that his mate should devote her life to his needs. Civilisations are mostly built on slavery and women are more often than not the willing slaves because of the way they have been brought up.

All animals of the same species, and all birds of the same species, seem to have an inbuilt pattern of behaviour. For instance I am told that all English blackbirds will choose a territory, sing to attract a female, help her to choose a nest-site, but leave it to her to build the nest and incubate the eggs. The male bird takes no turn at incubating the eggs, but does help to feed the young when they are hatched.

Each species seems to have this inborn programme even when they are unlikely to have seen any adult behaviour which might influence them. Cuckoos all throw out the eggs and nestlings of any bird in whose nest they have been laid as eggs. Then they migrate to North Africa when fully fledged, which must be programmed behaviour.

In very few species do the males take any interest in feeding and bringing up the young. There are a few exceptions like one species of fish which drives the female away when the eggs are laid and looks after them and the fry himself.

Then there are those peculiar creatures called sea-horses which are really fish and probably of the same species as pipe-fish, where the male becomes pregnant. The female passes thousands of eggs into the male pouch and then goes away having done her bit, and the eggs are nurtured and fed like any foetuses in a womb by the male sea-horse, until they are ready to be born and then the sea-horse gives birth to thousands of little replicas of himself who then go off and fend for themselves. Most, of course, end up as food for predators.

But doe rabbits and polar bears and others have to have their young well away from the males who may kill them. Lions will kill the cubs of a previous head of a pride and the lionesses do not seem to try to stop them. Apparently the lionesses do the hunting for food and then the lions take "the lion's share" and if there is not enough to go round the cubs starve. Some men have been said to resemble lions.

All of mankind is one species; so, as most men seem to behave in the same sort of way, is it that their behaviour is an inborn programme like the animal and bird species? I am sure that they would like to think that it is.

Many male and female animals only come together at mating time and lead quite separate lives during the rest of the year. Mankind unlike most of the rest of the animals has an all-year round mating and breeding time, but the only times that a good many wives see their husbands is at meal times or in bed. Otherwise they mostly lead separate lives.

The men spend their free time apart from work, at their clubs or pubs, golf clubs, cricket clubs, fishing, or at football matches etc., while the women stay at home and look after the children that is, while the children are small. If a man has a hobby, and his wife or girl friend wants to see anything of him, she has to support his hobby, be it games, steam engines or whatever. Very few men will interest themselves in a woman's hobby unless by chance there is money in it.

Men seem to like being regimented, and like joining clubs with silly rituals as if they have never grown up. And have they? They also like getting drunk together and acting in a stupid rowdy manner. Drunkenness in men is tolerated far more than it should be. But men think that women should never get drunk. That is a male preserve. Women do not normally see any fun in getting drunk but some do take to the bottle at home when they can no longer put up with their frustrations. But how often do you hear of a drunken woman driver killing someone on the roads?

Women (in the main) are forced to grow up to raise their children. They often find that they have to treat their husbands like spoiled children (holding the purse strings) because that is the way his mother still treats him and that is what he likes.

If he can afford it he allows himself high-priced toys like new cars, motor cycles (or even planes if wealthy) but often thinks his wife should be content with a piece of jewellery. How often do you see the man with a new car which he uses just to go to work, while his wife takes and fetches the children from school and does the shopping and all the errands in an elderly car?

EQUALITY OF THE SEXES

Women will never achieve any sore of equality with men while they treat their sons and daughters in unequal ways. Equality should start in the home and women have themselves (and LIFE) to blame if they never achieve it. The Jesuits used to say

"Give me a child until he is seven and he is mine for the rest of his life" or words to that effect. Mothers usually have their sons for longer than that (except for the rich who send them away to boarding school) and it is up to them and the fathers of the children to teach their sons and daughters that they all have equal rights and should respect each other's rights.

This teaching sometimes will not be easy, as the mother will have to deal with her own feelings of partiality towards her sons, and perhaps the opposition of her husband if he has been brought up to think that he is a member of the only half of the human race worth considering.

I think that boys should be taught how to clean a house, how to cook, wash and iron and do the shopping and should practice doing it just as much as the girls. At least they will never think that a house runs itself, and everything else just does itself. It is a shock for some men when they are left to look after themselves when their wife dies or leaves them.

If a woman idolises her sons she will in turn idolise her grandsons and thus perpetuate the inequality. But in time given that they are not sabotaged by too many "I'm all right Jills" (who say they do not want equality probably because they already have a private income and so are in any case independent) women should achieve a lot more than any Parliamentary laws can do, particularly when they are not being enforced if they give women any advantage however slight, over men. Men will outwit women every time if they can turn the law to their advantage, and ignore the law if they cannot.

If a woman had murdered thirteen men before being caught, there would have been an outcry. But Sutcliffe was not apprehended because after all he was only murdering women, so there was an exceptional degree of police incompetence. This may have been because some of the women were prostitutes, but they were still women and should have been protected. Just because they expect to be paid for sex does not make them any less women. If a woman had murdered thirteen men who used prostitutes the outcry would have been just as vociferous.

Men took the opportunity of the "Equal Opportunities Act" to take some of the top jobs that had previously been considered women's jobs, such as hospital matrons (now dubbed senior nursing officers or Hospital administrators) and Heads of Girls' Public schools and State schools and colleges. Where are the women who have made any inroads in these male spheres? Where is the Headmistress of any Boys' Public school, or vice-chancellor of a University. Women can do any of these jobs as well as any man given the opportunity. Mrs Thatcher was Prime Minister longer than any man this century. There have been and still are women Prime Ministers of other countries, and no one can say that they were any worse than any of the men at the job. But women have to have faith in their fellow women and encourage their daughters to take up any of the few professions that men will allow them to invade, and do something positive about making men give way about other jobs, otherwise most women will still get nothing except the lowest paid and most monotonous jobs that men do not want.

Things alter for a little while when there is a war or a shortage of young males and women are recruited to do men's jobs. But when the war is over the women are sent back to their kitchens. They achieve no equality. They are just made use of in any crisis.

Because of the way they have been conditioned, few women will go to a woman lawyer, trust a woman air-plane pilot, ship's captain, or even a woman bus driver (until they have experienced the smoother ride.) Unfortunately there seem to be few women bus drivers because most of them cannot take the harassment they get from the male drivers in the garages. Other countries have women pilots and ship's captains so they have proved that they are up to the job. Other countries also have far more women judges than this country has.

Prime Minister John Major's "Opportunity 2000, the Employment Initiative for Women" did not get off to a good start. No Employment Minister was present at the launch. The 1990 Report of the Hansard Society Commission chaired by Lady Howe, concluded that women have still to be much better than male candidates to win promotion. The Annual New Earnings Survey showed that 16 years after the Equal Opportunities Act the average wage of female manual and white-collar workers remains at its 1975 level, two-thirds of male wages. In America women have gone much further ahead. The International Women's forum do not intend to include Britain in its future plans. They say "You are in the dark ages as far as women are concerned."

I am sure that what most women want must be financial independence, which in these days most of them had had before they had the children, if they had a job. It must be very galling for a woman to have to ask man for money that he considers is his because he earns it at work, especially if he is by nature tight-fisted, and more especially if he is no longer in love with his partner. Many marriages and liaisons founder over money problems.

A woman's work in the home is unpaid. A wife comes cheaper than a housekeeper. Because women work for nothing except their keep in the home, women's work in every sphere is undervalued and underpaid. Women will have to refuse to work for nothing, remembering that anything that is free has no value in many people's eyes. It is only services that have to be paid for that are esteemed. Even in the Koran, the Holy book of Islam, I am told that a wife's duty is to sleep with her husband and bear him children but she can demand payment for anything else. I do not suppose that anyone has actually demanded payment, but it does prove that wages for housework is not a new idea.

Women subscribe to the view that their work is worth very little when they engage other women to do their housework or look after their children. They pay as little as possible, not realising that by doing so they are undermining their own position in a man's world. They expect, and have to pay the male plumber, gas fitter, electrician, car mechanic etc., etc. a goodly sum because they know he will not come if they do not, but they expect any women to be satisfied with a pittance. How short-sighted can women get?

I realise that women's dependence on men is because they need a breadwinner to support them and their children while the children are young, so women's careers get interrupted and they never catch up with the men. Or they can only start a career when the children have grown up which is bit late in the rat race. All this makes achieving any equality in a man's world very difficult. It seems that women have to remain single or at least childless. With surrogate motherhood that may alter.

Women who are single parents either from choice or because they have been deserted by the father of the child or children, have a very thin time unless they have a private income. Their children too are deprived of many things that other children have, as well as being deprived of a father. A man, when at work, has a domestic life to return to, his wife and children. A woman should also have a domestic life to return to, a husband, children and a housekeeper, preferably an older woman, or perhaps a male, otherwise she will try to do two jobs all day and every day. Many working women do do two jobs and their husbands let them.

PUTTING WOMEN IN THE PICTURE: A QUESTION OF GENDER

I admit I lose my patience
(Said the fat man in the bar)
When I hear the wife complaining
How exploited women are,
I've attempted to convince her
Though alas, to no avail,
That the female of the species
Is inferior to the male

They were born to be supportive
They're not fit to have control,
For the destiny of women
Is to play a minor role,
They should bow to man the master,
Be content to be his slave,
And rejoice that every semi-
Is a prehistoric cave.

Every Jane should thus acknowledge,
As her Tarzan beats his chest,
That it's nice to be woman,
But to be man is best.

If her fate is to look sexy,
Or be called a stupid cow.
Let her dream of liberation,
In a thousand years from now.''*

WOMEN AND CHILDREN

Women have a compulsion, it seems to have children and continue the human race. LIFE's motto being "survive and breed" women instinctively try to find the best provider for their children that they can in the circumstances in which they find themselves. I suppose that is why women are not so influenced by good looks as men seem to be in their choice of a partner. It may be that men's preference for good looks and good figures is one of LIFE's ploys to ensure healthy generations. In the animal world the male does the displaying and the female does the choosing, and presumably she chooses the strongest looking.

WOMEN DESERTED BY THEIR HUSBANDS; AND WIDOWS

For many wives there is the constant threat that their husbands will leave them after say twenty years of marriage for a newer model, someone as young or even younger than their daughters. This seems to be happening more frequently in all walks of life. The wife's chance of attracting another mate are

---

*By Roger Woddis by permission of the author and the Radio Times.

slimmer than her husband's as most men want women younger than themselves to prove how virile they are.

Then, if the wife has no income of her own, or has not been able to pursue a career, she is left on her own to bring up the children (if any) without a home, because it has to be sold and the proceeds divided between husband and wife. She may have no means of support except Social Security or Income Support or whatever name is now given to it, if she cannot get a job, unless her ex-husband agrees to pay maintenance which most men say they cannot pay when they set up a second home. Thus, she loses, at one go: her home, her status, her standard of living, her sexual life and probably her social life. Women on their own do not get invited even to dinner parties in the same way that couples and single men do.

Women should learn two lessons from these everyday facts. They should not be in too much of a hurry to have children, and they should train for the best job they can manage before they have the children, so that they have something to fall back on if they are divorced or widowed.

BRINGING UP CHILDREN

They are more likely to enjoy their children if they have given themselves time to have whatever is their idea of a good time before becoming mothers (which is a job for life,) and are less likely to get "four-walls-itis" that sense of being imprisoned by the children and the daily chores. Also, they may realise that bringing up the children and making a happy home is the only job that really matters. But it is a job, and usually a very demanding one so that most women need to get away from it for short or long periods (according to temperament) and do something completely different, pursue a hobby, or at least meet new people whose entire conversation is not about home and children.

However, nothing at all in anyone's later life will ever have so much influence as the love and care they got during their first ten years of life, or the lack of that love and care. "We are all our childhood writ large"

Our childhood seems to be the longest part of our lives no matter how long we live. Just think of all the well-known people that you have heard of, whose lives have been warped by their childhood experiences. Your childhood influences everything you do in later life. We forget when we grow up how what we thought were injustices endured in our childhood, are still influencing us. The miseries we knew are still with us, being bullied at school, snubbed, rejected, accused of crimes we did not commit. These things have made us what we are. We even feel that we might have been better human beings if we had been treated with more kindness, justice and love.

When it comes to bringing up our own children, most of us choose to forget what it was like to be a child and we treat our children as we ourselves were treated, or neglect to ensure that they do not have to endure the miseries that we endured. We say of any tragic happening "Children soon forget" when if we only take the trouble to look back to the events of our own childhood, we would know that children never forget, just as we have never forgotten, and what is more, children frighten themselves with all sorts of imaginary horrors if they are not told what is really happening.

I think we expect too much of mothers today and give too little support. Mothers have to fill a whole series of roles once provided (for some) by aunts and uncles and grandparents when most families lived in closer proximity. Of course some still do. I am thinking of the ones who are isolated from their families.

A lot of the drudgery of housework has been taken out of housework but it still has to be done, and the shopping done, and the meals cooked while still looking after the children. Mothers can no longer send them out to play in safety in our seemingly violent society.

Although there are fewer children, the responsibility for them still rests on the mother. Fathers will often admit that they hardly knew their children as persons until they grew up.

Parents love their children, usually, more that their children love them (except in their very early years.) They in turn will love their children. Most parents greatest difficulty is in acknowledging that their children are adult and no longer need their guidance. Children cannot realise how difficult it is to be a parent until they become parents themselves.

When a man is left to raise his children because his wife has died, or because she has left him, and he is not well enough off to afford a housekeeper, he either marries again very quickly or puts his children into "care". In exceptional cases he gives up his job to manage the chores and bring up the children. Very rarely does he stay at work and raise the family at the same time. But women are supposed to do just that when they have no husband and to do it on far less money than a man gets, and usually without the female help he gets from his mother, sisters, or neighbours with his washing and cleaning. And society, both men and women think it is no more than a woman should do.

WOMEN'S BEHAVIOUR TOWARDS WOMEN

Because of their idolatry of their sons, some women will do terrible things to their daughters things that they would never do to their boys. In China, the mothers used to bind the feet of their baby girls and break the arches with a stone (the ones they kept, the ones that were not exposed for the beasts to eat.) This binding broke all the bones in the feet and the girls screamed in agony and could never dance or run again, and only walked with difficulty. The mothers did this because that was the way that their sons wanted their wives to be, unable to run away when they were ill-treated. This is not all so long ago and far away. If you go to China today you may even see old women tottering about on their little stumps of feet.

Today, the mothers and grandmothers in some Arab and African countries will horribly sexually mutilate their young daughters and granddaughters by cutting out the clitoris (often without any anaesthetic) so that the girls will never have any pleasure from sexual intercourse, because that is how their sons want their wives to be. They call this female circumcision instead of what it is, sexual mutilation. There was a B.B.C. 2 programme about this subject in March 1983 in the programme "40 minutes" - "Female circumcision." I think it should be shown again. There are still young women coming to Britain who have been thus mutilated.

They also cut the girl's vagina and stitch it up so that the cuts grow into one flesh, and leave such a small opening that girls have to be ripped or cut apart on their wedding night. There have been reported cases of doctors being asked to do this to brides in the U.K.

These barbaric practices lead to all sorts of infections. The menstrual flow cannot get away, and in some cases it may take a woman an hour to empty her bladder depending on how much the vagina and surrounding tissue has been closed up. All this of course makes childbirth even more painful and dangerous because of the scar tissues from the cuts and joins, and because the woman usually has to be cut open to have the child. If women stopped doing these terrible things to their girl children, the practice would die out at once. No-one can cite any religious pretext for these mutilations. Millions of women are mutilated in this way. I can only conclude that women do not like women. They prefer to slavishly obey the wishes of men.

Women tend to be wary of other women, and rightly so. The other woman may attract the partner or perspective partner away. Most men are likely to roam given the chance. Needless to say women roam as well, but they usually have fewer opportunities, especially when their children are young. Many women do have strong friendships with other women (I am not talking about lesbians) but even in these friendships there is still a wariness until the age when it no longer seems to matter. How many women have found their husbands having an affair with their best friends? Nevertheless, most women's friendships with other women are likely to be deeper than many of men's friendships with other men. Men's friendships are often pub friends, golf friends, fishing friends etc., but not many whole-life friends. I wonder why?

A lot of women can be very jealous of their daughters even if they never admit it openly. Sometimes it is because their husbands make more fuss of their daughters than they do of their wives. Queen Victoria is reputed to have been very jealous of her eldest daughter Victoria because Prince Albert loved her so much. She was quite happy for her to be married off at the age of just seventeen to the heir to the German Empire, and Queen Victoria wrote her very loving and comforting letters when she was no longer an ever present rival for Prince Albert's affections.

Women can be very jealous of their daughter's looks and youth especially if they were once very beautiful. Conversely they may be very proud of their beautiful daughters, if they are everything their mothers had wished for themselves when young. Men too can be just as jealous of their sons for various reasons.

Sometimes both parents are proud of their offspring and sometimes both parents loathe them. Pretty well-formed children stand a better chance of engaging their parents' affection. Edith Sitwell was one such unfortunate. Her beautiful mother, married at eighteen, gave birth to Edith at nineteen and was devastated because she was not the beautiful daughter she was expecting, and ignored her for the rest of her life.

LANGUAGE

> "The continuing use of the masculine to express truths about humanity, and the feminine only to particularise the female has contributed to the ideology that women are different, worse than separate, just peripheral."
> (Author unknown)

This is exactly what I have been doing because there is no pronoun for him/her and he/she. Language itself is loaded against women. The very word woman derives from man, and female from male as if they are of a lesser species.

All history books tell us that men did this and men did that, with no mention of women at all. We are told "man embraces woman" well, we know he does, but is that just an excuse to leave out half of the human race? An Act of Parliament in 1805 insisted that the word "He" stood for "she". In most children's minds, the word "man" just means the male and not the female.

A TITLE FOR WOMEN?

Men do not have to declare their marital status. They are all Mister unless ennobled. A woman is either "Miss" unmarried or "Mrs" married. Some women do call themselves Ms but that is usually assumed to mean that they are either single or divorced. What women need is a handle that divulges as little as Mr does.

In days gone by, all women married or single were called "Mistress" but that would not do with to-day's connotation of the word. The only mistresses allowed are school mistresses or in the phrase "mistress of her craft" etc.

What I suggest is that, as all gatherings of men and women are usually addressed as "Ladies and Gentlemen" all women should call themselves "Lady" which would not imply single or marital status. All those whose present title is already "Lady" could be given some other title.

A former member of Parliament Dr Edith Summerskill, objected to women having to change their names to that of their husband's but somehow the idea did not catch on with the general public. Perhaps now is the time for the change with so many divorced women around. If women do not return to their maiden names, which itself is a nuisance as so many documents etc., have to be changed, they can find that they are duplicates. I believe Mrs Margaret Thatcher was a duplicate before her husband's previous wife married again.

Men quite like to be called "Sir" in shops and restaurants and when in a position of authority, but few women like to be called "Madam." Sir derives from "Sire" but Madam derives from "my dame." It sounds better to us with a French accent but it is actually *ma dame*, my dame.

"Madam" has been demeaned by common usage. Madam is the head of a brothel, a keeper of a bawdy house. It is also used of unruly little girls; she is a proper little "madam." Nobody has ever said of an unruly little boy, he is a proper little "Sir." Once again I think we should change "Madam" to "Lady." Now only the market traders call a woman "Lady" when they don't call her "duck." Royal ladies and women in authority are usually called "Ma-am" which is once again just an abbreviation of "Madam." They too should find another title.

In the same way, giving the title "Dame" to women of distinction is more than ludicrous as common usage has diminished the original meaning. I know that dictionaries say that "Dame" is a title given to women of authority etc., but that is no longer the accepted meaning of the word. We associate "Dame" with dame-schools and most of all with men in drag playing the Dame in pantomime. In the song from the American musical South Pacific "There is nothing like a dame" I do not think it means a woman of authority. I think a more becoming title should be found for those ladies who are supposed to be honoured.

"When honoured a man adds "Sir" to his name.

A woman becomes a pantomime "Dame."

WOMEN AND SLIMMING

Some young women and girls no longer enjoy food. No, all most of them think of is how many inches each mouthful will put on their figures. They are all slimming to the point of anorexia to be like the skinny models they see on the fashion cat-walks and the skinny successful women they see on T.V. and films. When they have slimmed down to as near to a skeleton as they can manage, they then wear the baggiest clothes anybody has ever worn. What is the point of the slimming? It is a sort of bondage that women have taken upon themselves. Why?

Men do not bother. Their beer bellies hang out everywhere. It makes women into frightful bores. I am sure this semi-starvation affects their brains and bones as well as their bodies. Slimming is an industry making millions of pounds out of women's credulity. It is all so pointless. Their bodies metabolise more slowly to compensate for the reduced food supply and then if they start to eat their normal amount of food they will put on more pounds than they ever lost. I am not against those who are really obese eating a lot less if their condition is not due to some glandular malfunction, but there does seem something obscene about millions of women subjecting themselves to silly expensive slimming diets (to the benefit of the manufacturers) when millions in the world are really starving. Why can't they just eat less if they want to look skinny, and shut up about it. Slimming to excess leads to anorexia and bulimia (gorging on food and then causing oneself to vomit so that no nutriment reaches the body).

According to the American Anorexia and Bulimia Association, 150,000 American women die of anorexia every year. It has reached epidemic proportions but because it makes women docile, nothing is attempted to prevent it.

It is suggested that it was started in America by dropping the official weight figures for women one stone below most women's natural level, thus making women feel that they were too fat and therefore failures. A major industry was born, dieting and diets.

When women starved themselves so that their breasts almost disappeared, they then had cosmetic surgery, silicon breast implants to make them look like normal women. Breast implants are a good thing for women who have had to have breast surgery but quite unnecessary for others. As Naomi Wolf says in her book *The Beauty Myth*:

> "Dieting is the most potent political sedative in women's history. A quietly mad female population is a tractable one. It is a direct solution to the dangers posed by the women's movement and their economic and reproductive freedom."

THE POSSIBLE FUTURE OF WOMEN

Now that it is possible to detect the sex of the child before birth, parents will be able to choose which sex they want and abort the others. This will at least prevent the killing of live girl babies where the parents only want boys. One abortion clinic is reputed to have carried out 6,000 abortions of which only one was male. When all the peoples of the world can have the choice, and they mostly choose boys, how will the girls then be regarded? Will they be sold off to the highest bidder? Will they be prized and cosseted? Or will they, like the Tibetans (I am told) have to be wife to all the sons of the family so that their life will be even harder?

There is one thing for sure, it will reduce the populations of the worlds unless the men use the women to continually breed. Men will not restrain their sexual appetites as women are expected to do when war has killed off their prospective partners; so will the women of the future be treated like the women of Islam? Kept in domestic captivity, not allowed to drive cars, or travel except with their men-folk, wear tent-like cover-up garments, never speak to any men outside their immediate family, barred from the law and medicine, the teaching of male children etc. etc. and the introduction of temporary marriages which seems to be an Islamic version of prostitution. Single women who refuse a temporary marriage could risk prosecution for having an "anti-Islamic attitude."

ONE SEX WORLD?

If "Cloning" is really feasible, men could invent a future without any women at all. (Cloning is said to be the reproduction of the whole animal or human from a few cells of that animal, as each cell is supposed to contain D.N.A. the instructions for reproducing the whole body.) If it can be done, we know that it will be done.

All the men would be homosexual because they would still have sex on the brain just as they have now. This would be no novelty for some of those who have been in all male-boarding schools, prisons etc.

On the other hand the same could apply to an all female world. Or we could even discover how aphids and other insects can procreate females without the help of males. Bees do it. When they want males they apparently produce a few drones to fly with and fertilize the queens of other hives. How do they do it? Of course the Queen bee has had a nuptial flight so that is how she is able to produce males. Aphids seem to produce males when they want variations. In some animals, shrimps for instance, the older females can turn into males when needed. Both of these worlds would be very different but probably no happier. The male world might even exterminate itself without the restraining effect of women. There would also be no variations, no new people, only replicas of the ones already there. All clones would succumb to the same diseases.

How do shrimps change one sex into another without any operations? Many women would opt to be men if it was known how to do it in this man's world.

CHAPTER IV

MARRIAGE

"The value of marriage is not adults produce children but that children produce adults."
Peter de Vries

"Marriage is a bribe to make a housekeeper think she is a householder."
Thornton Wilder

"By the time you swear you're his,
Shivering and sighing,
And he vows his passion is,
Infinite, undying,
Lady, make a note of this,
One of you is lying."
Dorothy Parker

Both men and women seem to expect too much of marriage. It is amazing that so many marriages last so long when you consider how very little men and women understand about one another. We are all supposed to have a masculine side and a feminine side, which should help somewhat in understanding our different natures. But, although men and women may have been brought up in the same sort of families and gone to the same schools their biological rhythms (plus the boy's and man's preferential treatment) makes them very different.

A man cannot really know what it is like to be a woman and a woman cannot know what it is really like to be a man, which is why very few male writers can make the heroines credible to women, and very few women writers can conjure up male characters that men can believe in.

The men who have so-called sex changes are usually opting for what they see as the easier life, without ever having to put up with the tensions and hormonal upset caused by menstruation, childbirth and the menopause, with all their discomforts and accompanying mood changes. They are really neuters, just pretend women, having been brought up with all of the privileges of being male and none of the relegations of being female. Many of them do think that they are in the wrong bodies which is why they have the sex change.

This difference in the make-up of the sexes is best illustrated by the sort of magazines which each sex buys and reads. The publishers gear their products to maximum profits, so the men's magazines are full of nubile young women or even pornography, men's sports, mechanical gadgets, photography, and of course, cars. Any stories in the magazines are usually violent and aggressive.

Whereas the women's magazines are full of impossible romantic stories with fantasy men of the kind never to be found on this Earth; plus innumerable articles on: make-up, hair, slimming, fashion, cookery, housekeeping, child-care, and how to get your man without whom no woman's life is deemed to be complete. They have recently become more informative about sex, abortion, child abuse etc. - subjects that used to be entirely taboo.

The only hobbies women are supposed to have are domestic ones such as sewing, knitting, embroidery, decorating their houses, gardening, and perhaps art and music; if they have any talent and time to fit them in.

The magazine proprietors are in business to make money so they evidently supply what men and women want, or what most of them want. There are of course "minority-magazines" for those interested in other subjects, but these are not so lucrative so they are always an endangered species.

What people choose to read tells you a lot about their attitudes towards themselves and the rest of the world. Newspapers cater more for men than for women so are mainly bought by men. Nearly every newspaper has pages devoted to men's sport, football, racing, golf etc., etc. Women's sport may get a small paragraph sometimes; men are not interested in reading about women's activities.

Men do sometimes condescend to watch women's tennis. Despite what the Australian, Cash, said about women's tennis, it is usually more interesting to watch than the men's game. We do get rallies. Men's professional tennis mostly consists of unreturnable serves. If men in professional tennis were only allowed one serve instead of two the game might be more interesting. Those who felt on form would still try out their rocket serves but we would actually get rallies from those who felt a little less confident.

There are quite a few women who have bets on horses especially since the advent of betting shops, but most of the gambling is done by men. They have the money.

Many wives have no idea how much their husbands spend on gambling. In fact, many women have no idea what exactly their husbands do at work, or how much they get for doing it, although marriage is supposed to be a partnership. Some women will say that they are quite content not to know as long as their husbands give them enough housekeeping money to pay the bills and clothe the children etc. As the man is usually the one who earns the money he naturally thinks he is entitled to what he needs for smoking, drinking and gambling, and he would probably be infuriated if his wife asked for the same amount for the same activities. I doubt if she would get it.

Marriages (except arranged marriages like that of the Prince of Wales to Diana Spencer) are supposed to occur because the participants are in love with one another. Who was the Frenchman who said: "There is always one who loves, and one who is loved"? Marriages seem to last longer if the husband is the one who loves.

Both parties really have to settle for who is available. A few men can marry the boss's daughter, but most of us have to stick to our own class, the poor to the poor, the middle-class to the middle-class and the old money to the old money.

Many women marry because they want children. Some marry to get away from oppressive conditions at home and then find that they have jumped out of the frying pan into the fire. Men marry for sex and a home of their own.

LOVE

Some people think that love in marriage has only existed since romantic novels came to be written, but love stories have existed all through the ages. Yet not all marriages were love marriages. Where marriage was the only way by which women could have a home, women have settled for a loveless marriage and accepted whoever asked them.

Nearly all of us have experienced the pleasures and pains of falling in love. When we are young we are always falling in love and falling out of love, and seeing our beloved through rosy spectacles. We cannot see them as they really are. We are really in love with love. This is really a biological hallucination by LIFE for the propagation of the species. As the old saw has it "love is a dream and marriage is the alarm clock." And so it often is when couples fall in love and do not give themselves time to know one another and become loving friends. But sometimes, even after knowing one another for years, couples find, when they marry, that they have married strangers. This is fine if they have more than physical attraction between them and can learn to love one another with the surprises entailed in getting to know one another. But if physical attraction is the only lure, boredom with the marriage soon sets in. Noel Coward (who was a homosexual) said: "loving is more important than being in love. If one leads to the other you are in for a long run."

Even if a couple have lived together before marrying they sometimes find that marriage changes their attitude towards one another. They may feel more owned, or more free to argue or throw a tantrum, or quarrel, because they think their partner cannot so easily walk away as when they were living together without any legal tie. There are some couples who thrive on rows and think a peaceful marriage is insipid. I cannot believe those who say, "they have never had a cross word." I can only think they have never voiced an honest opinion. On the other hand marriage may give couples a feeling of greater responsibility for one another. I think couples should marry when they become parents. Even in this age 'bastard' is still a term of abuse. And children do need two parents.

Every marriage is different and nobody except the couple concerned can really know what their marriage is like. And sometimes not even the participants know. How often do we read of men or women whose partners have walked away, saying that they had no idea that anything was wrong. This is usually because of a lack of communication. The couple have got out of the habit of talking to one another. One of them, or both of them, are too busy or just not interested.

Marriage seems to be more popular than ever, even if the married couples are longing to be free; the single ones are longing to be married. Judging by the number of people willing to try again after a failed marriage, it must seem to them that being married is the only way to live. Dr Samuel Johnson said: "A second marriage is a triumph of hope over experience." But even he would have married again if Mrs Thrale would have had him!

There is one thing for sure about any marriage, neither partner should ever admit to being unfaithful. Furthermore, neither partner should ever tell of any sexual experience with anyone else before the marriage. Even if a divorce is in the offing, it will be less acrimonious if neither knows that they have been betrayed. If the marriage continues, sexual experience before and extra marital experience will be remembered during every row, and unforgettable insults will be hurled.

There are some who think that marriages fail because divorce has been made too easy. Those who have endured a divorce think that it is still a traumatic experience that they could well have done without. Now that the law allows divorce after only twelve months of marriage, there should probably be another law to make marriage more difficult. Perhaps a law to say that they cannot marry until they have lived together for twelve months, and that if they have children they must marry and not divorce until the children are sixteen years old. Hard luck! But they might exercise a bit more care before bringing fatherless children into the world. Then there are those who should never marry. They are temperamentally unsuited to living in a close relationship with anyone. Nevertheless, some of them do marry out of loneliness.

Women are not usually as able as men are to walk out of an unsuitable marriage, because they are not usually financially independent, and also they may be more devoted to their children. Yet, we are told, seven out of ten divorces are instigated by women. Are more men going off with someone younger, or are women getting fed up with the way men treat them? There have been some programmes on T.V. about marriage and men's and women's different attitudes. On a Channel Four programme, most of the men (working class) referred to "the wife" or "the missus." None of the wives said "the husband," or "the Mr." An Australian said he had married a Phillipino girl because she would be more amenable and loving than an Australian girl, and she was also more beautiful. A Phillipino girl said that all that the men wanted were beautiful girls as housekeepers and bedmates who would leave the men free to do exactly as they wanted without question.

On another programme, young unmarried Englishmen said they wanted wives who would be content, but they did not say what they should be content with. They all seemed to want wives like the robots the women had been turned into in that sinister film *The Stepford Wives* (book by Ira Levin) or perhaps the nearer reality of the brain-washed wives in the sequel to that film.

One man said of sex: "As long as I have a good time, I don't care how she feels. Women have periods and they are the greatest turn-off. They should keep it to themselves and not bother us. They should stick to women's things, housekeeping and bringing up the kids."

The women said, "You are expected to live his life, and follow his hobbies. He will laugh at, and ridicule any of yours." Another woman said "You are his joke, the wife." Yet another woman: "You are there for him to take his frustrations out on. He will be furious if you are in any way more successful than he is, especially if you make more money. Men expect you to wait on them just like their mothers did. They expect to go on drinking and gambling just like they did before they got married." I do not think that any of these were exactly successful marriages.

It is true that many men do find it difficult to remain married to women who are more successful than they are. Mr Denis Thatcher was cited as one who managed it when his wife was Prime Minister. But remember he is still a millionaire, and money is real power.

Barney Blackley wrote:

> "Most women get married, it's true;
> They think it's the best they can do.
> But why spend your life
> Being somebody's wife
> When you might spend it just being you?"

CHAPTER V

MANKIND

Why is there only one species of mankind? We all know that all mankind can interbreed. They may have different coloured skins, be pygmies or tall, have curly hair or straight hair etc. but they are all one species. There are thousands of species of most insects and many species of most animals (or there have been) but only one species of man.

So, why has man managed to dominate this planet? He is not a fast runner like some animals. He has no protective armour. He is not bigger. He is not stronger. Because of his nakedness man was obviously programmed only to live in warmer climes. He has stolen the furs of other animal and the wool of sheep and goats and learnt to make clothes from plants like cotton and flax, before inventing nylon etc. It is because he has been given a better brain? Or is it an ability to learn from past events? Or was it because he was not frightened of fire, and turned it to his advantage to frighten off other animals? Fire probably originated in lightning strikes. Or was it because he invented weapons? Or was it because he was more ruthless and killed more readily, and not just for food? Some other animals do seem to kill for pleasure. Seals will kill penguins even when they do not want to eat them. But no animal kills as ruthlessly as man.

SPEECH

We do not know in which part of the Earth man originated. We all have the same sort of brain with the same sort of speech centre in the brain, so many of man's many languages have the same sort of sentence structure. Who invented speech? How was it invented? And why was speech invented? Most animals do not seem to need it. You may now cite whales and dolphins which appear to talk to one another in an altogether different sort of language. They have to communicate with one another over great oceans.

INSTINCTS LOST BY MAN

In his long history man seems to have lost some attributes that other animals and birds still have. He no longer seems to have a homing instinct. We know that cats and dogs and pigeons can find their way back home from enormous distances, even when they have been transported in cars or even in boxes, and in the dark to places unknown to them. How do they do it? And why cannot we do it? We must have been able to do it at some time. Birds migrate for thousands of miles, some quite alone, like cuckoos who have never even known their parents. They fly to North Africa. How do they know where to go, and how do they navigate? We must have been given the same knowledge at one time. Pigeons, bees, cats, dogs and dolphins etc., seem to have deposits of magnetite, a magnetic oxide of iron in their bodies. It has been said that man also has a concentration of magnetics in the base of his skull, so why cannot we navigate except with the help of maps?

TELEPATHY

Animals, while lacking speech seem to be able to communicate with one another. Perhaps they do it by telepathy. We have all experienced this if we have owned a dog. If it is something the dog is interested in, it can read our thoughts. Things like getting up and going to the door a few minutes before its owner returns if it knows that it will be taken for a walk. The time of return may vary from day to day, but the dog will still get up before it could possibly hear its owner returning. The dog can read your mind, but you cannot read his. We all retain some vestige of telepathy when we think of a friend or relation, and then shortly they visit or telephone. A thought has been transferred; but most of us cannot do it when we wish.

OTHER INSTINCTS

Some people still retain a biological clock that tells them the time almost to the minute at any time of day or night. Most of us have lost even that. Again there are those who know the points of the compass (even when they are underground.) All animals must have this knowledge to migrate.

FINDING WATER

Most of us can find water with a forked stick or even a couple of umbrella spokes. Of course, some have never tried so they do not know that they can do it. It may be that animals with long horns or antlers use them to find water. No-one knows how dowsing (water divining) works but there are lots of theories. Some dowsers say they can find metals or even dead bodies but I have never met anyone who could actually do this.

SWIMMING

We seem to have lost our ability to swim. We have to be taught to swim or else we drown. (There are always a few exceptions, those who swim the first time they enter the water). Most animals swim without any tuition. I am told that new-born babies swim naturally at once as soon as they are born. I have only seen this in a television programme.

HYPNOTISM

It is said that some animals transfix their victims by hypnotising them, so making them immobile. Many people can hypnotise others if they try and if the other person is willing to be hypnotised. Hypnotism has probably been used for many centuries as a pain reliever. The ones who are most easily hypnotised are those who can relax and fall asleep easily, anywhere. Insomniacs are the most difficult people to hypnotise.

Nobody really knows how it works. It is supposed to be autosuggestion (but usually by another person) but we cannot make our bodies become weightless unless the suggestion does come from another person. There are those who say they can hypnotise themselves, but I have yet to see one become weightless. Perhaps someone is working on why we cannot become weightless from our own suggestions, and defy gravity. We can become weightless for a very short period of time in a training "space vehicle" (known as a "vomit comet!) I do not know how long anyone can remain weightless under hypnosis. I presume that scientists who are investigating the effect of weightlessness in space on the human body, such as alterations in bones and muscles are also investigating the weightless hypnotised.

PHEROMES

Civilised people seem to have mainly abandoned Life's pheromes, the natural smell of the males and females which acts to attract the sexes to one another.

Recently, it was reported in some papers, a group of academics, cookery writers, and food fanatics heard how the aroma of human sexual pheromes is identical to that of some French cheeses. And that wines of the Smillion grape have been scientifically matched with the smell of a slightly sweating female underarm. Female moths are said to have pheromes that will attract males for miles around. As their mating time is so short Life has arranged for them to advertise their presence over a wide area. Other insects do this too, and man has tried to get rid of some of them that he regards as a threat to his crops, by attracting the male insects with the smell of the female, and then irradiating the males, thus sterilising them, and thus reducing what he considers to be the pest population.

Animals and insects must recognise one another mostly by smell. Some do not recognise their own reflections in a mirror or pool of water so how do they even know what their own species look like? Also the males and females often do not resemble each other at all, the females being much smaller and even of a different colour.

Then there are the different species who never even saw their parents, such as the turtles, the butterflies and all the others whose eggs are left to hatch without parental supervision.

Civilised man (or mostly women) have tried during the last few years (influenced by the advertisers of the products) to eradicate their natural smells, with great advantage to the perfume and deodorant manufacturers, who probably initiated the practice in the first place.

They have had less success with the men. Underarm body odour is supposed to be repellent and does seem so on the unwashed, but I have noticed that some of the girls whom their colleagues considered smelly, have usually attracted more than their fair share of male admirers. There have been primitive tribes who have forbidden their wives to wash their underarms.

In times past, when village dances were for the village girls and boys, (mostly farmhands) the boys used to put a clean handkerchief under their arm-pits to hand to the girls when they got overheated from the dance, because they believed that the smell of the handkerchief would, in the modern idiom "turn them on"

Doctor Dodd of Warwick University discovered that the human arm-pit contains musk which we produce when we become sexually excited, and we all have receptors which can detect the smell and sexually excite us in turn; so the farm hands knew what they were doing. Doctor Dodd is, or was, synthesising human musk, and some perfume manufacturers aim to incorporate it in their deodorants instead of the musk of the tiny Nepalese deer which is now used. This can lead to fewer deer being killed just for their musk.

So, in the future we shall go on destroying our natural musk with deodorants and anointing ourselves with synthetic musk to attract the opposite sex.

MAN'S AWARENESS OF HIMSELF

Man has realised that he has a conscious mind and has been told he also has an unconscious mind. He has some knowledge of his past history, but only of the past 7,000 years, a very short period in man's history. He is also aware that he will one day die, although he must live as if he thinks he is immortal.

We do not know, and cannot know if animals and insects know that they will die. We have seen that when animals are dying they hide themselves away from their own kind. Is this because they know that others will finish them off if they find them? We do know that animals and birds kill off any of their own kind that are weak and feeble and unable to look after themselves, including their own children. The runt of the family is often left to starve.

MAN'S INVENTIONS

Man has invented the wheel (probably after seeing boulders rolling down a hill) agriculture, cooking, music, mathematics, speech and writing, radio, television, computers, space travel etc., etc.

We do not know when in man's history the first of these inventions were discovered. The earliest records we have show them to be in a very advanced state. The composers of music we most admire usually cannot tell us where their music comes from. A lot of man's inventions appear out of the blue, or when man was trying to invent something quite different, and they often come to more than one person at about the same time. In the last hundred years there have been more inventions and discoveries than in all the recorded history of mankind.

Computers, robots etc. could, in the future ensure that only those who wanted to work would do so, while the rest enjoyed a life of leisure (given that provision is made for the non-workers to be able to live a reasonable life out of the profits of the workers) or alternatively everybody could work just a few days or hours in every week. Needless to say no Utopia like this would ever come to pass. The rich will go on getting richer and the poor will get still poorer.

MANKIND AND THE PLANET EARTH

We all know that we are destroying this planet and using up all of its natural resources for short term profits for just a few people.

We know that tropical forests are being destroyed to produce pasture land that will become desert in a very short time because the top soil is very poor and only the long roots of trees can find any nourishment.

There are reported to be many species of animals and insects and plants living in the tropical forests that man has never seen and now may never see.

Nobody knows yet what the effects on the world's climate will be when all the forests have gone, but there are some dire predictions.

We are allowing all the populations of the world to expand and push all the other living creatures off the Earth. We cannot recreate them when we have killed off the last one or rather two.

We are polluting the land and the seas. Some of the wastes, especially the radioactive wastes will last for thousands of years. They may never decay. We have no right to despoil the Earth for future generations (if any). Until fairly recently I suppose we could claim that we did not know what we were doing to the Earth, and all the diverse plants and animals, but now we cannot help but know, and still we let the destruction go on. I do not know how we can prevent it while every nation can do what it likes with its own land. "The United Nations" is not strong enough or powerful enough, or perhaps not even willing enough to put an end to it.

Some Governments are getting together to discuss the problems but perhaps it is already too late.

In the U.K. we have all noticed that birds and butterflies are getting rarer. I have seen it blamed on the increased number of magpies, but I think the shortage lies mainly with all the millions of gardeners, as well as the farmers. I cannot see the farmers giving up spraying the countryside with pesticides, so it is up to all the gardeners to give the birds and insects a chance to survive.

Many of us spray all the vegetation in our gardens with poisons including endemic poisons that ensure that no insect or caterpillar shall live, and thus we deprive the birds of their chief source of food on which to feed their young, and also we have no butterflies. Many also put down poisons for slugs and snails; then the birds eating the poisoned pests die of the poison. Thus poison kills just a few slugs or snails whereas if no poison was used the birds would rid us of thousands of them. Some even put worm poison on their lawns and deprive the blackbirds of their chief source of food while poisoning the birds. And if anyone could persuade the Italians and the French to give up killing off the song-birds that migrate over their countries, that would be a minor miracle.

CHAPTER VI

OUR WORLD IN THE UNIVERSE

No-one knows how or why the Universe began. There have been many theories, including the steady state, the expanding Universe, and now the most popular theory, the Big Bang. This is when and where all the galaxies are supposed to have been formed, and Time started. But you never get something out of nothing, so where did all the gases and dust etc., which are supposed to have formed the stars and the galaxies after the Big Bang, come from in the first place? And why was there supposed to have been a Big Bang?

And this little planet we live on and call the Earth was formed out of the dust etc,. So, there was this spinning ball, the Earth, with enormous seas (why salty? and whence came the seas?) and a vast mass of land which eventually broke up (or was broken up) and drifted round the seas for a few million years until the continents we know today were formed. Certainly they look as if they might once have fitted together like a jigsaw puzzle. And this Earth spun round on its axis (how come all planets and stars have an axis to spin on?) once every twenty-four hours only 94 million miles or so from the star we call the Sun, thus giving the Earth night and day (except for the North and South Poles).

The Earth also spins in an elliptical yearly orbit round the Sun, thus giving us our seasons of spring, summer, autumn and winter according to how near or far we are from the Sun. All the other planets of our Sun supposedly formed at the same time as the planet Earth, each spin round their individual axis giving varying lengths of day and night for that planet, and each has its own yearly orbit round the Sun. Venus's orbit makes its day longer than its year. This we call our Solar system, Sol being the Sun. The Sun presumably has no knowledge of the planets that are dependent on it.

Now, supposedly there are millions of Solar systems in the Universe, and they are all kept hanging or rushing through space by gravitation, as we are told. We know that Sir Isaac Newton formulated the known laws of gravitation but who created gravitation? What Cosmic joker is responsible for the whole Universe? Our Galaxy alone is said to have more than two million stars (who counted them?) and nobody can even guess at the number of galaxies.

Our planet Earth has collected a small, dead, secondary planet we call the moon, which somehow got caught up in the Earth's gravitation. This moon's own gravitation, as it spins on its own axis has a great effect on the Earth, causing among other things, the tides of the seas. (Why are some seas tideless?) It also has an effect on every living thing on the Earth. It may have something to do with the salt in the seas and the salt in blood. Who knows? Women's monthly menstruation cycle is roughly the same as the moon's cycle. Everybody's moods are partly governed by the moon. We acknowledge this influence when we dub people lunatics (from Lunar, the Moon), who, it has always been thought, are affected by the full moon.

There is theory (which once again cannot be proved or disapproved) that the Earth once had an earlier and smaller moon, which owing to some collision broke up on the Earth, forming perhaps the Iron Mountains of Abyssinia, Russia, and elsewhere, and probably causing the land masses to buckle into mountains. We know that parts of the Rocky Mountains of Canada and the Andes and parts of the Himalayas were once at sea level. Sea shells have been found in many places and there is a salt water lake in the Andes.

This collision of the Earth and the moon could have put the sea-shore on the top of the mountain formed by the collision. Before the supposed break-up of the moon on the Earth and probably others asteroids as well, the size and gravitation of the Earth would be much less, which would account for the enormous trees, ferns and animals (such as dinosaurs) which would able to grow so much larger when their weight was so much in comparison with our present level of gravitation.

These enormous plants and trees formed our coal-mines miles underground with the vegetation having no time to rot down. The likely theory for this can only be cataclysmic collisions. A complete tree has fairly recently been dug up from a deep mine. People are now more aware of fossils so they would take note of it, whereas before it would have been ignored.

There is new evidence that a meteorite struck the Earth 65 million years ago in Tibet. This is indicated by ashes of forests and high concentrations of platinum and iridium, so scientists tell us.

Our present moon has a gravity said to be six times less than that of the Earth. We have seen on our T.V. screens how easily men in terrifically heavy space suits can leap about on the moon's surface, so the reason the dinosaurs and enormous plants disappeared could be the increased gravity. It is also believed by some people that the description of the creation of the Earth in Genesis, the first book of the Bible is what is remembered by mankind of the breaking up of this moon and the eventual acquisition of our present moon. All known religions and myths allude to floods which could have covered most of the Earth and been the aftermath of these cataclysmic events. It may even be that myths about giants are really remembered from times when the Earth's gravitation was less and men grew large like the animals and plants.

The more we learn about ancient civilisations, the more we realise that man has been around for far longer than we ever thought, perhaps even millions and millions of years. It may be that ancient man was not so very different from the man of today, except for the technological breakthrough which has altered our life-styles; but most of us would have great difficulty in explaining anything about this technological breakthrough to anyone. We can use the machines but we do not know how they work.

Many of todays' inventions could have been invented before and been lost and forgotten when civilisations were destroyed by barbarians, and libraries burnt, and entire populations wiped out in the constant wars that mankind has waged. Certainly all the inventions were there waiting to be discovered. All the now-known laws of physics and chemistry were there (if they are laws and not theories to fit what we know at the present time)

Man's recorded history only goes back about 7,000 years. Why? Did some catastrophic event wipe out all previous records, but not man himself? Mankind has survived.

There is yet another theory that the rotation of the Earth has been affected in the past, perhaps by passing comets, or the alteration in the orbits of other planets, causing them to come closer to the Earth and this it is believed has caused the Earth to turn upside down. There have been recorded instances of the Sun rising in the West and setting in the East a few hundred years ago, so our solar system may not be as stable as we imagine or hope. The fall of Jericho may even be one such turnover. Similar events are said to have been recorded in Chinese history.

We know that the ancient writings and languages of about 7,000 years ago are so intricate and complex that they could not have possibly been man's first attempts.

Most of us are now fairly used to the idea that our entire Earth is just as big as a grain of sand in comparison with the surmised immensity of the Universe. And that there are living organisms so small that even our most powerful electronic microscopes are not yet good enough to define them. We see Eternity and Infinity stretching in both directions, the too big to imagine and the too small to contemplate.

If we do not destroy our Earth with nuclear warfare somebody in the future might manage to unravel a few of the myriad mysteries of LIFE and the Universe. An American space probe passed one of the outermost planets of our solar system in 1989 and now we are told it will take 958,000 years to get near another star (if it lasts), by which time we may well have demolished the Earth. Of course the probe will probably miss all the stars by millions of years and just go on through space for ever until it disintegrates. We shall never know.

In July 1991 a Professor Andrew Lyne, head of a team of astronomers at Manchester University has deduced the existence of a hitherto unknown planet outside the Solar system which they think may be 12 times the size of the Earth but with the same surface temperature and capable of sustaining human life. Is this the one we head for when we had despoiled the Earth?

Sir Fred Hoyle does not believe in the Big Bang theory. He prefers a theory that the Universe is in a process of continuous creation.

Dr. Tom Broadhurst favours a theory that the Universe is

much smaller than others think it is. When he measured the distance between hundreds of faint galaxies he noticed a pattern emerging. The Universe seems to him to be like a giant beehive with galaxies clustered along the walls in a sort of cosmic honeycomb and astronomers keep seeing the same galaxies time and time again as light spirals back on itself in a hall of mirrors effect. The distance between the walls of each cell is about 420 million light years. This has delighted the sci-fi humorous author Douglas Adams, as give or take a few noughts 42 was the answer to the "Great Question of Life, the Universe and Everything" provided in Douglas Adam's book *The Hitch Hiker's Guide to the Galaxy*.

Here are some comments on the Universe by writers: Sacheverall Sitwell wrote:

> "If we are really alone in the Universe, without any other living creatures of whatever form this side of Eternity, then it is indeed more extraordinary that can be expressed in words. The whole of creation is too extraordinary for us to understand. It is indeed world without end in the comprehension and understanding of its wonders that could last not for one, but for a hundred lifetimes."

Dorothy Richardson wrote:

> "One might perhaps die of wonder if one could think hard enough over the fact of their being anything anywhere."

Thomas Carlyle, when he heard a contemporary, Margaret

Fuller, had said; "I accept the Universe" Commented, "Gad, she'd better." Nevertheless, many people fail to accept the Universe. They just refuse to think about it.

Dorothy Sayers said:

> "Most people would sooner die than think, and most of them do."

CHAPTER VII

RELIGION

When life gave man his larger brain and his awareness of the world around him, he instinctively felt that there must be some creator or Gods who had made all things, and to whom he must bow down and worship in the same manner that he had to behave with the man who had set himself up as leader or ruler of his people.

As he, like us could have no guidance on this matter, he probably worshipped the Sun which gave him warmth, and water both of which sustained him and the crops he grew. All this was very well until some men pretended to know more about the various Gods and spirits that he worshipped than other men did. Thus men invented religions, and when the religion makers were powerful enough, probably with the help of the said rulers, those that did not believe could be coerced by various means: force, threats etc., to believe or at least to behave as if they believed.

There have been many thousands of religions throughout history and there are many still today. Most of them have been the cause of much misery and cruelty, not to mention all the wars of which they have been the cause, and the religious wars still raging today. All of them have been too small in conception and too parochial to serve as a religion for all the world.

All rulers and Kings have needed the help of a religion to keep their peoples subject to their rule. The Christian religion was very suitable for this because as Karl Marx said: "The social principles of Christianity preach servility, cowardice, self-contempt, subjection and defeatism." Christianity also promised a life hereafter so that people could be treated badly in this life believing that they would get their just deserts in the next.

Very few self-styled Christians that I know have actually read the Bible on which their religion is founded. They have read bits of the Bible taken out of context, and heard somewhat incomprehensible verses read out in Church. If they would read *"The Bible designed to be read as literature"* (it should still be available in Public Libraries although long out of print) which leaves out all the text numbers, and repetitions and "begats" they might have some idea of the vindictive and vengeful God of the Old Testament. Remember the Old Testament is the basis of the Jewish religion and Jews do not accept the New Testament, and Jesus Christ as the new Messiah whom they were awaiting. Christians, followers of Christ, often forget that Jesus Christ was a Jew and so were all the apostles.

> "How odd of God,
> To choose the Jews. (anon)
> But not so odd
> As those that choose
> A Jewish God
> And Spurn the Jews."
> (Another anon)

"The story of the stories, the chosen people and its God" by Dan Jacobson, is an account of the Jews by a Jew, telling why he thinks the Jewish God had to be a vengeful God.

The Christian Church was founded by St. Peter and St. Paul supposedly on the teachings of Jesus Christ as reported in the Gospels. But the Church became the exact opposite of the teachings. It became rich and powerful, with a hierarchy of priests and with services conducted in a language (Latin) that very few people understood. At that time few people could read, so they had to believe whatever they heard in Church, whenever it was in a language that they could understand.

It is said that the Christian religion spread through Europe because a Roman Emperor (Constantine?) was undecided between the Turkish Sun-God and the God of the Christian Church. He invoked the latter and won the battle he was engaged in, so Rome adopted the Christian Church. It was probably more complicated than that but Rome did adopt the Christian religion. Bamber Gascoigne wrote a book called *The Christians* a history of how the faith spread. This was made into a T.V. programme. Dora Russell's book *The Religion of the Machine age* is about the baleful effect religion has had on the social systems of the Christian West and the Orthodox East.

THE GOSPELS OF THE NEW TESTAMENT

All we know about Jesus Christ is contained in the Gospels, none of them written during his lifetime so they are all different in their accounts of his life and teachings.

St. Matthew, writes of the house that the wise men visited to see the baby Jesus (note house, not stable). It is the only one of the Gospels to write of Herod killing the first-born, and Joseph taking Mary and the baby to live in Egypt until Herod died. Then nothing more is said of Jesus until he comes to John the Baptist to be baptised.

St. Mark does not mention the birth and starts with the baptism. St. Luke says that Mary was cousin to Elizabeth, the mother of John the Baptist. This time the baby is laid in a manger because there was no room at the Inn. Joseph and Mary had had to go to Bethlehem presumably for a census of inhabitants. There is no mention of any wise men visitors or of Herod killing the first-born or of the flight into Egypt, only of going each year to Jerusalem at the feast of the Passover. Then Jesus is baptised by John the Baptist and Jesus is said to be about thirty years old.

St. John also starts at the baptism by John. There is no suggestion anywhere that Jesus was born on December 25th, or that he died at Easter. These were two pagan festivals taken over by the Church, because otherwise they would have still been celebrated as before. There is no mention anywhere that Jesus was married. It was the custom of that time for Jewish boys to marry by the time they were nineteen, so he could have married and had a family. In the New Testament the only mention of marriage is in verse 30 St. Matth XXII, "For in the resurrection they neither marry nor are given in marriage." This was the answer to a very tricky question put by a woman who had been married in turn to eight brothers as each one had died. She had wanted to know whose wife she would be in the hereafter. Nowhere does Jesus preach against sex as sin. It was St. Paul who regarded sex as sin.

George Bernard Shaw, in his preface to the play *Androcles and the Lion* suggests that Jesus did not announce that he was the son of God until after his sojourn in the wilderness and that being alone in such a place for any length of time can have an adverse effect on peoples' brains or personalities.

At the end of the Gospels there is again conflict after the crucifixion. St. Matthew. "And the eleven disciples went away from Gallilee into a mountain where Jesus had appointed them, and when they saw they worshipped but some doubted." St. Mark. "Jesus himself stood in the midst of them, but they were terrified and affrighted and supposed they had seen a spirit and he said unto them "Behold my hands and feet that it is myself, handle me and see, for a spirit hath not flesh and bones as you see men have." And he showed them his hands and his feet. He said unto them "Have you any meat?" And they gave him a piece of a broiled fish and of an honeycomb and he took it and did eat before them. St. John "Jesus then cometh and taketh bread and giveth them the disciples and fish likewise. Now this is the third time Jesus showed himself to the disciples."

There is no suggestion anywhere here of a resurrection, only that Jesus was still alive after his terrible ordeal. Sir Zafrulla Khan, a former President of the International Court of Justice, wrote a book, *Deliverance from the Cross* (Pub. London Mosque) putting forward a theory that Jesus was revived by the ministrations of Joseph of Arithamathea and Nicodemus, and then went to India in search of the lost tribes.

Professor F.M. Hasnain, Formerly State Director of Archaeology in Kashmir, claims that he found the tomb of Jesus the Gatherer with a Christian cross and a slab of stone in which the sculptor had cut an outline of two feet pierced with holes. He also quotes a book, *Bhavishya Mahaa Purna* written in A.D. 115 which relates that a king travelling in the Himalayas forty years earlier, had met a man who said that he was the Son of God, and had suffered in a far country. I have no means of verifying any of these statements.

A preacher called Jesus probably did exist but the Gospels all give different accounts of what he preached, so the Church that grew up in his name could take any bits they pleased and leave the rest. As most of the population were illiterate they only knew what the priests told them of what was in the Bible.

There are contradictions in the character of Jesus as reported in the Gospels. Compare St. Matthew 5 v 2.

"Blessed are the meek for they shall inherit the earth." with St. John 2 v 15.

"When he had made a scourge of small cords he drove them (the merchants) out of the Temple." This is hardly the conduct of a meek man.

I do not know how the doctrine of "eternal damnation for sinners" is reconciled with "only believe and all your sins are forgiven" or "Jesus died for all the sins of the world."

At first the crucifixion was known as the shameful death and the subject was avoided by the Church. Eventually the Christian Church made the crucifixion the centre of the religion and adopted the symbol of the cross. If the execution had been by a hangman's noose would the symbol of the noose have been adopted by the Church? I doubt it. The cross, but not the crucifixion was the symbol of much older religions.

Eating the body and drinking the blood were old cannibal customs for acquiring the virtues and qualities of slain enemies, and this practice is continued in the "Communion" of the Christian Church.

The Catholic Church seems to be obsessed now with the barbaric crucifixion, and what it terms "the stations of the cross." Crucifixion was the most painful, dreadful, lingering death that the Romans could devise to stop any insurrections in any of their conquered lands. To the Romans, Jesus was a trouble maker.

The Church should have been concerned with what Christ was teaching, but of course no Church would be so concerned, as he was preaching something very like Socialism. The Church welcomed the idea of Heaven and Hell as a means of keeping the populations under control. The rich could buy absolutions for their sins from the Church and thus the Church became wealthy. More wealth was added by the tithes that everyone had to pay. Wealthy sinners also built churches to ensure their rise to Heaven. The God of the Christian Church had to be susceptible to bribery and bargaining, in the minds of the believers. "If I sacrifice something or other or crawl somewhere on my knees, then God will give me what I ask." It is only when the God has not kept what the believer thought was a bargain struck between God and himself, that the man has doubts about his belief.

The belief in Heaven and Hell was very strong for many centuries. The priests had done their work well. If we read Shakespeare's "Hamlet", in the "To be or not to be soliloquy" on suicide, we see that what restrains Hamlet is the thought of what might happen after death. His belief in the Devil, and the thought that what he had heard might be the Devil speaking when he heard the ghost of his father, also prevents him from taking vengeance on his uncle for his father's murder, until he has further proof that his uncle did kill his father. His proof comes when he learns that his uncle had also given orders for his, Hamlet's murder.

ST. PAUL AND SEX

St. Paul as the co-founder of the Christian Church seemed to be very anti-sex. This could have been because he expected a second coming of the Messiah and therefore new members of the human race were not wanted or necessary. But why should he think that when Jesus had been gone for so long, I do not know. 1st Epistle of St. Paul to the Corinthians.

VII verse 1: "It is good for a man not to touch a woman."

VII verse 77: "I would that all men were even as myself."

VII verse 8 : "I say therefore to the unmarried and widowed, it is good for them to abide even as I."

VII verse 9: "But if they cannot contain, let them marry for it is better to marry than burn."

So, the Pauline Church made people feel guilty about sex. Sex is sin. And that guilt still lingers with a great number of people.

MYTHS IN THE BIBLE

In the Bible myth of the Garden of Eden, Eve is supposed to be the one who is curious and desires knowledge, and so is tempted to eat of the fruit of the tree of knowledge. It was for this disobeying of God's command, that they were thrown out of the Garden of Eden. This myth makes woman responsible for the downfall of the human race, even though in the other myth she was only man's rib. Genesis 2 verse 22. Genesis 1 verse 27: So God created man in his own image, male and female created he them." So, the rib myth must be a later addition. In real life, men are the ones who are curious, and desire knowledge. Most of them will take anything to bits to see how it works.

Until fairly recent times, women were mostly denied knowledge unless they came from rich families with libraries and tutors.

If you believe the Adam and Eve myth about them being the first people on Earth you will have to believe the world was peopled by incest.

Why did men invent the myth of the first woman being formed from a man's rib? And the other myth of the Virgin birth? These are contradictory myths. In the one, the rib myth, man alone is responsible for the whole human race, which he knows is impossible. Are men so jealous that only women can give birth? In the Virgin birth myth, woman alone (without man) is responsible for the Son of the God he professes to worship. Here, men think that a woman is debased by having sexual intercourse with a man. There is nothing in the Bible that I know of that suggests the myth of the Immaculate conception, that is, that the Virgin Mary mother of Jesus, was herself born of a woman without sexual intercourse with a man. (Once again a woman would be debased by sex. Is this due to the teaching of St. Paul?) In one Gospel, Mary is said to be cousin to Elizabeth, the mother of John the Baptist. Even the word "virgin" is suspect in the Bible, it being said to be a faulty translation of young woman.

When Mary had borne a son who was said to be the Son of God she still had to follow the law of Moses. Leviticus 12 verse 2. which says that any woman giving birth to a male child is unclean for seven days, but in giving birth to a female child she is unclean for fourteen days. She must be purified for thirty-three days after the birth of a male child, but for sixty-six days after giving birth to a maid child, and give a sin offering to the priest for her atonement. For what sin was she supposed to be atoning? There was no suggestion that the father of the child had sinned. The child was not unclean. St. Luke. 2 verse 23: "The male child that breaks out of the womb is holy." Perhaps the law might originally have been formulated so that a woman who had given birth might not be pressed for sex until she had recovered from the birth, but it was debased into an insult to women. Jealousy again because only the woman could have a child? The Book of Common Prayer still carries this unclean insult in "The Churching of women", but the New Alternative prayer book omits it. And about time too.

FAITH

It has been said that "faith is the ability to believe in the incredible." Faith in a personal God is very comforting to many people, but when tragedy or disaster strikes, their belief is usually shaken. In reality, no-one can know LIFE, the creator of all things so there can be no worship, no ritual, no sacrifice, no bargaining and no bribery.

The Christian Church has been divided through time by many sects. The Catholics, the original sect, owe their allegiance to the Pope, and until recently conducted their services in Latin. Believers were, and are expected to believe everything the Church says, and to question nothing.

The Protestants protested at the wealth, and ritual, and power of the Church, and then came the Wesleyans, the Baptists, the Methodists, and all the other breakaway sects. Judging by the enmity between the Catholics and the Protestants in Northern Ireland at this time, they none of them ever seem to realise that they all believe in the same religion. But of course the real rift in Ireland is between the Irish, and the Protestant Scots who came over to Ireland at the time of the "Clearances."

When Henry VIII proclaimed himself head of the Church and broke away from the Pope in Rome because He would not agree to Henry's divorce from Katherine of Aragon, the Catholics were persecuted and burnt. His daughter Mary, a Catholic on her mother's side, burnt the Protestants at the stake as heretics. Then his daughter Elizabeth burnt the Catholics. I suppose she had good reason for they were forever plotting to oust her and put Mary, Queen of Scots on the throne.

In French history, Joan of Arc was given to the English by the Dauphin she had put on the French throne, when she was no longer winning battles for him, and she was burnt to death at the stake because she said she heard the voices of the Saints telling her what she should do, and the Church said that the Church and only the Church was in communication with God and the Saints, so she must have listened to the Devil. This was the basis of all heresy, usurping the power of the Church, and not acknowledging that all communication with God came only through the Church. Atheism, denial of the existence of God was also heresy, and the punishment was once again being burnt alive. I know little of other religions so I cannot discuss their Gods.

Buddhism seems different as there does not seem to be any God to be worshipped. All life should be respected. In your next reincarnation you may come back as some lowly animal or insect. You proceed by your virtues or otherwise through your many lives along the path of enlightenment until you lead the perfect life which leads to Nirvana - otherwise nothing, the end. What is the inducement to lead the perfect life? Also it is extremely difficult when you are an animal or insect as in Nature "there are no moral judgements; there are only consequences." I understand that Buddha was against any idols or even rituals or any sort of mumbo-jumbo, but enormous statues of him abound, and monasteries house Buddhist monks chanting in a language that no-one else understands.

In religions in general mankind is addicted to rituals. We invent them for every sort of occasion; after the ritual has been performed more than twice it becomes a tradition and lives for evermore. An essential of all religions seems to be some sort of mumbo-jumbo. A lot of people do think that if they cannot understand it, it must mean something profound, but like Grand opera when it is translated into language that they do understand the triviality is apparent. Of course scientists and doctors use the same device to mystify people. Lawyers, of course are adept.

Most religions include a life after death for humans only. "Man's only hope of immortality is his belief in it." About life after death Bernard Shaw wrote:

> "Heaven as conventionally conceived is a place so inane, so dull, so useless, so miserable, that nobody has ever ventured to describe a whole day in Heaven although plenty of people have described a day at the seaside."

Why should man think he is immortal? All of Earth's teeming living creatures and plants are made of the same building blocks, the so-called amino acids and electrical charges, so if mankind is immortal so is every plant, bird, insect, fish, animal, bacteria, virus, and every living thing. But, says man, "he has a soul." Where? And who says man has a soul? Why, man himself! Who is the you that expects to live forever? The brain damaged, the mutilated in war or by accident, the senile? The personality altered by drugs, chemicals, operations or disease? When the body dies, that is it, *finito*.

We all live for a very short space of time, seventy years or a little more if we are lucky. We were not here for millions of years before that so what is so different about being dead for millions of years after our little life? Of course the belief in an after life of everlasting bliss (or Hell) was fostered because people could be exploited and repressed in this life if they thought all would be well for them in the next world.

Karl Marx said:

> "Religion is the opium of the people. It enables us to bear what otherwise would be unbearable, and because it makes the sickness of society bearable, it removes the motives to cure and the will to cure." Was he right? Now that so many people no longer believe in any religion or any Church, will anything change for the better?

Samuel Butler said:

> "All the animals except man know that the principal business of life is to enjoy it." Obviously he had never really observed any wild animals who think the principal business in life is to get enough to eat and perpetuate their species.

CHAPTER VIII

CIVILISATION AND GOVERNMENTS

Many civilisations may have started as dictatorships, with the strongest (and perhaps the greediest) dictator electing himself as leader or ruler, taking the land and enslaving the inhabitants.

At one time it was thought that the Euphrates Valley, in ancient Mesopotamia (now Iraq) was the "cradle of civilisation" but now South East Asia may have had one of the first civilisations. Archaeologists have found evidence of even earlier civilisations in Thailand. The Romanians may have developed a written language before the Mesopotamians. There may have been no one "cradle of civilisation." Different civilisations could have occurred all over that world.

Eventually, even in a dictatorship there would have to be a willingness for people to live in some sort of harmony with one another and to band together against enemies. Most civilisations seem to have been built on slave labour. (I am told that it is a myth that slavery has been abolished. There are today in various parts of the world as many people in slavery as there ever were in times gone by).

Men have by war, been able to grab the land for themselves and have given chunks of it to those who helped them in their conquests, and these rulers and landowners have gone on through the centuries owning the land which should belong to all of Earth's inhabitants.

The civilisation, the society in which we live, makes hypocrites of most of us; as we conform, more or less, to the acceptable behaviour of that society. The behaviour displayed, changes somewhat with each new generation of adults. Civilisation can only flourish if we all agree to obey certain rules and have faith that others will obey the same rules. We all have to have faith in say, bus drivers, airline pilots, doctors, surgeons and any others into whose hands we entrust our lives.

We also have to have faith in the people who are governing the country, although that faith is constantly undermined by the knowledge that the Government mostly operates in secret and often against the interest of the common people, and makes its own secret rules so that those people cannot find out what is really going on.

Speculation has been rife among ordinary people about many things. Such as how was it that Lord Kitchener (of the First World War) was in a ship going to Russia when Russia had been out of the war for about two years? And was it not providential that there was only one survivor to tell the tale when the ship went down? And has anybody ever seen a monument to Lord Kitchener? And did Hess mistime his visit to Britain? After all most of the aristocracy had already disappeared to America for the duration so Lord Hamilton had no choice but to hand him over to the Government. And why had we always been told that the Russians wished to keep him in solitary confinement? Wasn't it that he could name names and not Russian names? And did he live too long for somebody?

And during the Profumo scandal, was it not strange that Stephen Ward committed suicide? He was not the type. Was he about to become indiscreet? The Royal ladies all became pregnant at this time and those babies are all now 27 years old. This is all a long time ago but some people have long memories.

TAXES

The really rich, of course can avoid obeying most of society's rules with impunity. They of course can even find ways of avoiding paying taxes to keep the country running. In the U.K. most taxes are paid by people on Pay-as-you-earn. The rest are indirect taxes on consumer goods and services, on which the poor are likely to pay the most as they are less likely to get discounts, free hospitality, company cars, free holidays (sometimes disguised as Conferences) and various other "perks", not to mention the "Golden handshake" when they quit a job.

Everybody hates paying taxes, especially if they do not agree with the way the money is spent, so that people will try if they get the chance, to pay as little as they can get away with. This is very difficult for those on P.A.Y.E. but seemingly easy for the highly paid who can go bankrupt or just cease trading if it is their own company, while owing many thousands of pounds to the Inland Revenue, and while they are still living in opulence in splendid mansions which are presumably in somebody else's name.

The really wealthy can salt their money away in Swiss banks or tax havens and in trusts so they pay no taxes or inheritance taxes.

Maximilien Robespierre wrote:

> "What is the origin of that inequality of means which concentrates all the wealth of a country in a few hands? Is it not to be found in bad laws, bad government and all the vices of a corrupt society?"

English society is dominated by the notion that it is superior to be, rather than actually to do anything. Achievement in business is pointed towards arriving at a financial position where further striving is unnecessary. Those who have been in a position to do nothing for a long time become of course, the upper classes, the aristocrats, the gentry, who can afford to look down on the *nouveau riche* and everybody else. Money talks, and old money talks the loudest.

Every civilisation is riddled with class systems. The working class hoping that their offspring will become middle class (and forgetting that they will then probably disown their parents through snobbery) and the middle classes hoping to move further up the hierarchy and everyone looking down on those they think are lower in the social structure. Snobbery is rife everywhere.

America was supposed to be a classless society, but we hear of the "Four hundred" a list of "the best families" in America. As John Collins Bossidy wrote:

> "And this is good old Boston,
> The home of the bean and the cod,
> Where the Lowells talk to the Cabots,
> And the Cabots talk only to God."

CHAPTER IX

EDUCATION

It seems to me that almost nothing I learned at school with the exception of English grammar and literature has ever been of the slightest use to me during my life. I learned to read and write before I went to school (at a later age than most children) so I do not count those skills, but perhaps I should count elementary arithmetic as being of practical use. School and everyday life seemed to be different spheres having little in common.

The history I learned was mainly of kings and rulers and was slanted of course towards making Britain the centre of the world, and of course always in the right. Every country slants its history that way. History is mostly fiction, because we rarely get to know what was actually going on. If you lived through the 1939-1945 war as I did, how much did you really know of what was happening, apart from the bomb damage you saw and what the newspapers told you? Little smatterings of information have come out during the past years, but the whole truth is something we shall never know. When it is time for the archives to be opened they have always been "weeded"

How much of what is going on now do you really know? Newspapers have "D" notices or something similar under a different name which forbids them to print anything the Government does not want known such as reports on pollution etc., and you never know how much the news has been manipulated and by whom.

So as Henry Ford said: "History is bunk" perhaps not bunk, just fiction.

Dean Inge said:

> "What we know of the past is mostly not worth knowing. Events in the past may be roughly divided into those which never happened, and those which do not matter."

The geography that I learned has not fared much better. All the mountains and rivers are still there, but some of the forests have vanished and the names of many countries have changed. Even the counties of England have had their names changed together with their boundaries. The biology, chemistry, and physics taught were elementary and these sciences have certainly moved on, so my original stock of knowledge is practically useless.

I learnt some arithmetic, geometry, algebra and trigonometry, and have only ever used the arithmetic to do calculations which school children now do with their little calculators.

Of foreign languages we learned the grammar and found when we visited the countries we were quite unable to hold a conversation. We wrote essays but we were never encouraged to think for ourselves. If by any chance we came up with an unorthodox thought we were reproved. It was not done to question the accepted way of looking at events and beliefs.

WHAT FORM SHOULD EDUCATION TAKE TODAY?

It is obvious as automation takes over, and more and more of the jobs that men and women have spent their lives performing will vanish, probably millions of children now at school may never have a regular job except in service jobs which robots cannot do. The academically bright ones will still get into the professions, though these may get over-crowded, but the unskilled will have little choice.

So, what we should be teach them is how to enjoy life. After all their future will be mainly a life of leisure so they must be encouraged to make the most of it and not turn to crime from boredom. After all that is what life should really be all about, enjoying living. It is not about money (although you must have enough money to lead a comfortable life). Life is not really about possessions as people discover when they have been in danger of losing their lives. Ironically, the ones who have come nearest to dying are the ones who most appreciate living.

YOUR LIFE IS ALL YOU HAVE

At this time the Government is short-sightedly cutting back on amenities for children, when it should be expanding them to ensure a more contented population. There should be facilities enough so that every child can be taught to swim and have pools to swim in, learn to ride a horse, sail a boat, play a musical instrument, ice-skate, or any other enjoyable activity they might wish to take up. At present, some of these activities are only enjoyed by the children of parents who can afford them. Why should other children be deprived?

Learning to speak is most likely the cleverest thing you ever learned to do. We learn it mostly by imitation and the more children are talked to the sooner they learn. Some parents very rarely talk to their children, so when they go to school they are at a great disadvantage because their vocabulary is so small.

Young children have a greater capacity for learning than we give them credit for. They can be taught foreign languages at the same time that they are learning their mother tongue. Children of bi-lingual homes learn that way.

Many young children get bored playing in sand pits etc, and are eager to learn if someone will show them or teach them, in a way that is fun, and if they are not expected to concentrate for very long periods.

We have all seen children (on T.V. if not in life), children of only two years old, learning to play the violin, that most difficult of instruments, with the Japanese Sazuki method where the parent learns with the child.

But one thing is for sure, you cannot teach anyone anything if they do not wish to learn, but you can teach a child who does wish to learn almost anything, if it is taught with enthusiasm and real interest. Children can learn a lot from radio and television as long as someone keeps them away from their favourite rock music long enough for them to watch other programmes.

In school children should be taught the three "R"s, including correct English grammar and spelling as it looks as if English (or American) will be the world's second language, and at present many foreigners speak and write better English than many of the English themselves.

Most foreigners rate English literature highly, so we should ensure at least that our children have the opportunity to do likewise by providing them with plenty of clean copies of books, and not cutting down on the expenditure on Public Libraries and school libraries. Of course there are many children and adults who do not like reading. Once they have learnt to do it, that should be their choice and not something forced on them by lack of books.

As I have already said children can be taught to converse in foreign languages. This language teaching must continue well after the age of five years. Most of us only remember isolated incidents from before five years old, when we get older, so we could and do, forget languages learnt in our early childhood unless the tuition or the practice of the language continues.

Children should not spend their time learning formal grammar (except English grammar). That can come later when they have learned to think in the foreign tongue, when their vocabulary is large enough. Children pick up languages very quickly from other children so perhaps there should be many more holiday exchanges. More time should be spent studying the works of Nature while there are still some around, and less studying the works of man.

Every child should have the opportunity to try a variety of crafts before the last of the craftsmen die out. The time will come when people will want original objects, pictures etc., instead of the mass produced items that the manufacturers decide they should want.

CO-EDUCATION

Co-education in England does not seem to be much of a success from the girls' point of view. Dr. Arnold of Rugby School once thought he would take in girls, because girls, being brighter at an earlier age than boys, might incite the boys to work harder, but nothing came of this scheme. Most girls do better in single sex schools than ever they do in co-education schools. Of course there are exceptions. Teachers of both sexes admit that they give far more of their time to the boys in their classes, even when they are consciously trying to be fair to the girls. This is because the boys are more demanding, while constantly demeaning the girls. As one girl said, "You could be trying to tell the teacher that the school was on fire and the whole school could burn down before he or she would listen to you." Many teachers talk only to the boys and ignore the girls. Of course a lot of girls do not like to appear to be cleverer than the boys knowing that the boys like to appear superior. Many girls would like to do woodwork and metal work but not in the company of the boys who would jeer at them.

Boys should certainly be taught to cook because they may have to look after themselves at some time. But they should not be taught with the girls otherwise they will get the girls to do all the clearing up and the washing up. Girls have mostly been brought up to please the males.

This bias against girls even extends to the marking of schoolwork. If it is neat and tidy and thought to be by a boy it is praised. If it turns out to be a girl's work she may be told she is niggly. Girls are often naturally better at languages than boys so it is now suggested that boys get higher marks because it is not fair that girls have a natural advantage. But nothing is said about boys having a natural advantage when it comes to maths.

I think that boys and girls should certainly mix at school, but I cannot think of any subject where the boys would not hog the teacher's attention.

We see the same thing on our television screens. In many programmes the girls and women are just peripheral to the story.

In a discussion programme there is usually only one woman and three men, and they all feel free to interrupt her as soon as she starts to speak. If she interrupts one of them the chairman calls her to order.

Stephen Leacock, a Professor at MacGill university, Montreal and a well-known humorist in his day, wrote in a more serious piece:

> "Oxford as I see it 1922." "I have taught mixed classes in MacGill for twenty years. On the basis of that experience, co-education is a mistake. In physics and mathematical science women are below the standard of men, but in language and imaginative literature the women would be the better - if they were not in with the men. A girl at MacGill with men all about her sits silent for four years. In women only colleges they lift up their voices and discuss things openly in their classes.
> The deeper trouble is that the curriculum is aimed at a man's career. Women need a different curriculum."

That was in 1922. But not much seemed to have changed. Human nature does not change.

ACCENTS

In English society, a person is immediately classified by his accent. If all children were taught a B.B.C. announcer - English accent or a "public School" English accent it might be less possible to place people. Everyone realises that the best jobs go to the acceptable accents (except when really good brains are needed) I do not think that this would be the end of dialects as they would still be used in the home. George Bernard Shaw said this best in his play *Pygmalion* which was the story used for the musical *My Fair Lady*, in which an uneducated daughter of a dustman was taught to speak with an upper-class accent (but not it seems, to have been taught any English grammar at first) and was palmed off in Society as a social equal. In spite of this well-known plea for a society where no-one can be classed by their accent, I have yet to hear of any State schools giving elocution lessons to their pupils. In fact it has been suggested by educational pundits that children should continue to use the sloppy grammar and expressions of their family speech and should not be corrected even when it is obviously ungrammatical.

LESSONS

I have noticed one slight improvement in educational practice. Children are no longer required to write with their right hands when they are naturally left-handed as they were in my day. This practice turned many of them into stammerers and also made them ambidextrous. We know now that the speech centre in the brain can be on either side, and that writing should match, so it is now left to the child to decide which hand to use.

I have long held a theory that history in the first classes at school, should be taught backwards from today (I suppose that is what is known as current affairs for older children) then the children could ask their parents and grandparents about recent years.

Geography could be first taught starting with the district in which the school is situated with street maps made by the pupils showing shops and supermarkets and post offices, post boxes, public libraries, places of entertainment etc. and moving on to the local town before proceeding to the whole of the British

Isles, and the rest of the world.

I still think that pupils should learn the multiplication tables even though they are now allowed to use calculators. Judging by some recently published results of schoolchildren's examinations, teachers obviously do not teach their pupils that they never need to learn their "nine times" table. Perhaps they themselves have never realised that the sum always adds up to nine and all you need to do is make your total "nine." For example, three nines are 27 that is 2 + 7, four nines are 36 that is 3 + 6. The first figure is always one less than the multiplier.

Bishop Creighton said: "The one real object of education is to leave a child in the condition of continually asking questions."

There seems to be a lot in the newspapers about falling reading standards. I have found that teachers and librarians denigrate their best yet asset for teaching children to enjoy reading. I refer of course to Enid Blyton. Children do not notice all the faults that adults attribute to her books. They only know that they are "happy" books, and if you remember your childhood you were often in need of a bit of happiness when you got fed up with "Do this, don't do that, come here, go there" They are probably not suitable for ethnic children but they can read books about their own culture.

CHAPTER X

PAIN

We know that pain is life's way of telling us we should stop doing something, that there is something wrong. Some people hardly feel any pain at all and are likely to injure themselves because they do not feel anything. Sometimes they are hailed as brave, when actually they are insensitive to pain.

There is sometimes an exquisite ecstasy in the first moment of intense pain. I suppose that that was what those self-flagellating hermits were aiming at.

This is perhaps LIFE's way of mitigating the pain of being killed, which must go on as each animal, insect, fish slays another for food, in the chain of LIFE. But prolonged pain is another thing altogether. It can be so intense that we lose consciousness.

It is said that the brain itself manufactures an opiate which will sometimes alleviate pain. This brain opiate which is said to be akin to morphia, may operate when people are engaged in strenuous exercise which may be why joggers often feel they are on a "high" that is, they are exhilarated as they would be on certain drugs. These brain opiates have been named enkepholates. Apparently they are immediately digested in the body; some research has been done to find a drug that will prevent the enzymes in the stomach from digesting them so quickly, so that they can work as pain killers for a longer period. This may eventually enable these natural opiates to be used instead of morphia.

I think that too little is done to relieve pain for most people. Aspirin (originally derived from willow bark, but now synthesised) is still the best pain reliever for inflammation, but much more is called for to relieve the pain caused by operations, cancer etc. We know that those in hospitals and special hostels get the appropriate amount of drugs such as morphia for cancer (it does not matter about them becoming addicts when they have so little time to live.) But all those people who cannot afford to go into hostels will probably suffer agonies because they will not be given the drugs in sufficient quantities. It should be everyone's right to have painless illnesses (as far as possible) and certainly a painless death, regardless of whether they can pay.

Surgeons in hospitals often do not even visit the patients they have operated on. They may say that they do not have the time. So they often have no idea of the intense pain that they have caused their patients; and patients themselves will put on too brave a face when asked about pain. They do not like to admit that they cannot put up with the pain as well as being afraid to antagonise the surgeon by grumbling. When they are in hospital, people feel very vulnerable.

I did hear of one surgeon who himself had had an operation and realised what his patients had to endure, and decided to try to do something about it, but I have never heard of any developments.

It was reported that Leeds Infirmary were using the longer acting local anaesthetic bupivacaine as a continuous nerve block for relieving pain after operations. The patients did not get so much pain and there did not seem to be any ill effects.

There was one method reported in 1982 to have been in use for about 6 years to relieve pain suffered by patients recovering from chest surgery where lung or heart complications can occur. It was called cryo-analgesia and relieved pain by freezing nerves; a cold probe was applied directly to the nerves and a thirty second freezing period was sufficient to block the pain for a few weeks. It was said that it had also been used to relieve the pain caused by some cancers, arthritis, and some nervous diseases.

Why is that treatment not available to everyone? I should have thought that it would be available for the relief of shingles which is sometimes excruciatingly painful, and which does affect the nerves.

Many are always in pain after an operation because a nerve has been accidently severed. Some who have had amputations spend their lives in pain because of the severed nerves. Could not this treatment help them?

The oldest known pain relievers are hypnosis and acupuncture. Both are time-consuming and more likely to be used on the people who can pay for the time involved. But as many people can hypnotise other people there is no reason why an acquaintance of the sufferer cannot learn the simple methods of hypnosis to relieve pain. Of course this has to be attempted when the pain has abated, so that the sufferer can concentrate on something other than his pains. The hypnosis should prevent further pain for a certain period.

No-one knows how hypnosis works and those who set themselves up as experts are those who have practised it more often and more successfully. They do not know any more about the mystery of how and why it works than anyone else, they just know from their experience which people can achieve a trance-like state in which they are amenable to suggestions.

The Chinese invented acupuncture hundreds of years ago, and it seems to work as a pain reliever and as an anaesthetic. This is not a treatment for the amateur to attempt. A lot of training is needed to be able to put the needles in the right places.

There are those who profess to heal by the laying on of hands.

This practice is mentioned in the Bible so it is not new. Perhaps this is a kind of auto-suggestion. Maybe all healing is faith healing, faith in your doctor, but above all, faith in yourself that you will recover from whatever ails you.

MENSTRUATION

Menstruation is the dismantling of the preparations which take place in a woman's body every month to receive a fertilised egg. When the egg is not fertilised the thickened womb lining etc is rejected by the body, and discharged as menstrual blood. This monthly cycle continues until the menopause, when all the eggs that a woman has received at birth from her mother are used up and so she is no longer fertile and cannot become pregnant. The body then begins to discard some of the reproductive processes. The ovaries begin to shrivel and no longer produce the hormones which they previously produced. This is where hormone replacement can help a lot of women. The natural secretions of the vagina dry up so making sexual intercourse painful. If a woman has an hysterectomy and her ovaries are removed she becomes menopausal immediately no matter what her age. Normally the menopause occurs somewhere between the early forties and middle fifties. It is a natural process and cannot be prevented, but the symptoms can be alleviated.

Doctors, being mainly men (there are some women doctors now, but not enough of them) have always regarded women's pains with less consideration than they have given to men's pains. Many of them spend more time with men in the consulting room. If a woman is depressed she is, or perhaps was, just given tranquillisers; perhaps they are not handed out so freely now they are known to be very addictive. Usually no attempt is made to discover the cause of the depression (which could be overwork, semi-starvation and boredom, none of which the doctor could relieve,) but the cause could be pre-menstrual tension which affects most women in various ways and which can at times be incapacitating in its effects.

Owing to the efforts of some women doctors men are beginning to realise that the women who complain of this are not neurotic. Yet only now is some small effort being made to alleviate of the symptoms of menstruation; back-ache, stomach pains, vomiting, cramps caused by excessively powerful and frequent contractions of the womb (caused by perhaps an abnormal output of prostaglandins,) headaches a feeling of being bloated, and sore breasts. This pain has been described as "angina of the uterus" which goes on for forty plus years for many women. Men would not put up with this. Some women do not get this amount of discomfort, but they do get very bad-tempered. Women film stars were never filmed at this time, as like all other women, their hair went lank and if they were subject to spots this was the time that they erupted. Opera singers were not required to perform during their periods as they were liable to sing out-of-tune.

Until recently menstruation was a taboo subject. Women were expected to keep their pains to themselves, with the males of the family (except the husbands) never hearing the subject mentioned. In my mother's day it seemed to be something of which you should be ashamed if any male member of the family even suspected that you had a period. As throwaway sanitary towels had not been invented this was often very difficult. Women did not like, and still do not like, discussing this subject with a male doctor. They could be more frank with women doctors who may have had the same problems. The old remedy for period pains used to be gin, hence I suppose "Mother's ruin" meaning that women got addicted to it. Some women also used gin to try to give themselves a miscarriage or an abortion.

I have had Headmasters of comprehensive schools ask me, when their young women teachers took a day off at this time because they felt too ill to cope with rowdy classes, if they were just malingering?

THE MENOPAUSE

Hormone replacement therapy should be freely available to all women when they reach the menopause if they want it, and not just for those women that a doctor thinks need it. Also the symptoms of the menopause often last for years and not just for months, as some doctors believe, so the treatment should be given for the duration. It has been estimated that 30% of women in America in this category are on HRT, and as it has been in use there for over forty years, it should be considered a safe treatment. HRT relieves symptoms such as hot flushes, migraines, absent-mindedness, and deep depression. Some women go through the menopause with little trouble except for the hot flushes and the thinning of the bones, but others become impossible to live with in their misery.

HRT also halts brittle bone disease, and protects somewhat against heart disease, strokes and senility. HRT could keep many women out of hospital (especially for bone fractures caused by osteoporosis, thinning of the bones during and after the menopause) mental institutions, and the divorce courts. When it has been proved to be so beneficial in so many ways, why is the medical profession mostly against using it? Some say it may increase the risk of cancer, but offer no proof. The cost of giving women HRT is very small compared with cost of not giving it (in human misery alone). So why are doctors in Britain so reluctant to prescribe it? Male chauvinism? Or do they like women to suffer?

HRT may also be the answer to that dreadful depression that some women suffer after the birth of a child. That too is thought to be caused by a depletion of hormones. Some women have refused HRT because they suffered too much from pre-menstrual tension and bad menstrual periods, and with the old type of HRT women still do get periods. But with the new type pioneered in America this does not now occur so they too could benefit.

CHILDBIRTH

Childbirth, being always regarded as having little to do with men, has always been omitted from the history books except to say how many children an historic figure had, with usually no reference to the wife who had the children.

Women were supposed to keep the pains of childbirth to themselves, and usually had the help of a village crone at the birth. The better off had the local doctor, if there was one. Many women died in childbirth, and most of those that lived were so worn out with constant childbearing that their lives were short. Many became semi-invalids through internal disorders, caused by bearing many children, disorders which in this day can be corrected by surgery. At one time, Catholic men were given the choice when either the child or the mother could be saved, but not both, of which should live and which should die, and a great number apparently chose that the child should live.

It was not until the invention (or introduction) of chloroform that any attempt was made to alleviate the pains of childbirth. Doctors everywhere seemed to be against its use for this purpose. But when Queen Victoria insisted on trying it, other women who could pay for it could have it.

Most births took place at home before the 1948 Health Act. Most women could not afford to go into hospital. Now, (until the latest cuts in the National Health service, so that home births are being encouraged again because they are cheaper) every one was expected to have the baby in hospital, where if the labour was very long some sort of analgesic was given. Now every woman (unless medically unsuitable) should be able to have an epidural; an injection into part of the spinal column which renders birth painless. I do not know if midwives are allowed to give these injections for home births but they certainly should be. Of course there are some women who have their babies so easily that it is not necessary for them.

It has been said that being born is the most dangerous journey we shall ever take, that down the birth canal, the cervix. It is also a very traumatic experience for all of us, and as we are only used to the dark and very little noise in the womb, there should be no bright lights and very little noise at the birth, and certainly no newly-born should ever be slapped, or even washed except for seeing that breathing is not impeded by lightly cleansing the mouth, and gently wiping the eyes against infection. The baby should be given to the mother straight away and not be taken away to be washed etc. We still do not know how our birth affects our future life.

The process of inducing births (except when the mother's life is at stake) should not be allowed. The baby is programmed to come when it is ready for the world. Induction often leads to respiratory difficulties because the baby is not yet equipped to breathe.

Childbirth in a lying down position is reputed to have been introduced at the request of one of the Kings of France so that he could see what was going on when one of his mistresses was having a child. This may be just hearsay, but doctors certainly prefer women lying down because it is easier for them to see what is going on. The natural position for childbirth is squatting or sitting on a birthing stool which seems to have been the practice in days of old. Gravity should be some sort of help.

We are told that in some primitive societies men were so jealous that the women could produce babies, that they used to pretend that they had all the pains and their poor wives who were actually giving birth had to wait on them.

A well-known French doctor has had some women giving birth in waist-deep smallish pools of water, as a natural method of giving birth but I should not think that it is any substitute for an epidural.

For various medical reasons some women have had to have their babies by caesarian section (so called after Julius Caesar whose birth was reputed to have been the first such birth). This means cutting the woman open and extracting the baby and the placenta. Many women who had caesarian sections, complained that they had been given an injection which completely paralysed them so that they could not even blink an eyelid or make any sound, and then were given so little anaesthetic that they felt every incision etc. They were not believed and told that they had had a bad dream, but now some anaesthetists have admitted that they gave the women very little anaesthetic, because they thought it might possibly harm the baby. These women have been tortured but I have not heard of any compensation being offered.

Most husbands are interested and anxious during the birth of their first child, and some will agree to be present at the birth; but some appear to lose interest after the first birth, and spend their time on their normal pursuits during further births.

Women, in my mother's day were not supposed to be seen in public when they were pregnant, and nothing was ever mentioned until the baby was born. The birth was described as "a confinement" (a word meaning an imprisonment, a detention). Pregnant women, if referred to in newspapers were always "in an interesting condition." It was as if women should be ashamed of being pregnant, but should nevertheless have as many children as their husbands wanted. Many men blamed their wives for becoming pregnant when they did not want any more children, although the wives had no choice there being no contraception available to them.

Some men have admitted that they dislike their wives when they bulged even thought they were the cause of the bulge. A man could tell a woman "Darling you have the most wonderful figure" and then do his best to spoil it, and dislike the result.

This prudery about pregnancy applied also of course to sex. It was never mentioned and it was surprising how many young girls were quite ignorant about it. Barbara Cartland in one of her interviews told of a friend of her young days (a young girl) who got married and was so shocked at what her husband tried to do that she went home to her mother. This at least proves that sex education in schools is a good thing.

"The midwife shouts 'Push 'arder!
I can see 'is little 'ead!
Me 'usband says all trembly like,
'I should 'ave stayed in bed!
I gives 'is 'and a squeeze and says.
'Don't fret me 'oney bun!
It's women's lot to bear the pain,
And man's to 'ave the fun!"
'Is face goes sort of whitish,
An 'is knees begin to knock,
I begs the nurse to bring more gas,
To ease 'is state of shock;
And when at last the baby comes,
I does the job real neat,
While the midwife 'elps me 'usband,
Who 'as fainted at 'er feet."
Written by Sue Denim.

CHAPTER XI

CONTRACEPTION AND ABORTION

The ancient Greeks and Romans all knew something about contraception, using various substances to prevent the sperm from reaching the ova but, judging by the enormous families the Victorians had, most of them knew little about the subject.

Since the A.I.D.S. scare condoms have been advocated by the Government as the principal method of contraception that should be used. But because the condom or sheath slightly lessens a man's enjoyment of sex, and is a bit of a nuisance, many men still think that a woman should take full responsibility for not becoming pregnant. They are not interested in the fact that the Pill does not suit every woman and can have serious ill-health problems for others. The Pill makes some women very depressed and uninterested in sex. Nobody knows the effect of a woman taking the Pill all of her fertile life.

Also the interuterine devices that some women use may cause bleeding and pain. No-one knows how they work but it is thought that they help the body to produce more prostaglandin which prevents conception. Some devices fail because the woman is not told that aspirin will destroy the prostaglandin and render the device useless at the time of taking the aspirin. The condom will not only protect both partners against A.I.D.S. (acquired immune deficiency syndrome) but also against V.D. and hepatitis B and also prevent the man from giving the woman cancer of the cervix, so it is thought.

Catholic women are only supposed to have sex when they do not want it, because that is the time of their monthly cycle when they are unlikely to conceive.

"It is now quite lawful for a Catholic woman to avoid pregnancy by a resort to mathematics, though she is still forbidden to resort to physics and chemistry."
H.L. Mencken

Men can enjoy sex at any time, but most women need to be at a particular time of their monthly cycle, and also to be emotionally involved (of course this does not apply to prostitutes who offer sex as a job with no emotion attached.) A man expects to have an orgasm every time but many women, though married for years, have no idea what an orgasm is. Children can be conceived without a female orgasm.

It is said that a new vaccine against pregnancy is being tried on women in India to reduce the population. It is supposed to work for two years. The population is said to increase by about 1700,000 each year.

A condom for women has been made but I do not know if it is in use. It seems to be a polyurethane bag which fits loosely inside the vagina and it is thought that women would rather trust themselves with birth control than pin their faith on men.

> There was a young man from Leghorne
> Who wished he had never been born,
> He wouldn't have been, if his father had seen,
> That the end of his condom was torn."
> Author unknown

When the Governments of all countries realise that the Earth can only support a certain number of people, even when it has pushed most of the animals to extinction, they will all have to make strict regulations about how many children anyone can be allowed to have.

This will be a great erosion of personal liberty but surely preferable to the wars for living space which will otherwise ensue. Wars to seize other Nations's territories and anhililate the inhabitants have always gone on, but they will be as nothing in comparison with future wars if populations are not limited. Remember there is supposed to be a neutron bomb that destroys people but leaves buildings standing.

Only when (and if) this fact is realised will public opinion welcome the "abortion pill" A French pharmaceutical firm has produced such a pill, R.U.486 developed in the eighties which allows women to have early abortions at four to five weeks. At present surgical abortion cannot be carried out until the eighth week of pregnancy. It has been approved by the N.H.S. so should be available on prescription. Treatment with the pill prostaglandin-based is carried out under medical supervision so the cost is probably more than for a surgical abortion, but this will probably change in the future. A simpler pill will have to be found if the whole world is going to have to use it. Of course the anti-abortionists may still succeed in banning it. I cannot see any difference between preventing the sperm from entering the ova, and discarding the fertilised egg before it has a chance to turn into a human being.

After all many such eggs are discarded naturally by every woman during her monthly cycles.

The anti-abortionists think that every potential human life should be saved even if it is subsequently extinguished by brutality or starvation.

So far the abortion pill is more expensive for the occasional use it will have, than the contraceptive pill which has to be taken daily. When a simpler pill is produced that could be used without supervision it should be the end of the daily use of a contraceptive except for the condom for preventing the spread of diseases. It should also be the end of abortion clinics except for exceptional cases.

In ancient times infanticide was an accepted method of population control. Illegitimate children and legitimate girl babies may have been killed. In the fourth century in Greece and then in Rome, infanticide was made illegal but it still flourished elsewhere.

Sealing children in walls, the foundations of buildings and bridges to strengthen the structure was common from the building of the walls of Jericho to as late as 1843 in Germany.

The practice of swaddling to deprive a baby of all movement lasted until the end of the eighteenth century. It produced a baby that was inert and passive. Read *The history of childhood* edited by Lloyd de Mause, Souvenir Press. It tells of the cruelties inflicted on children through the ages.

SINGLE WOMEN AND MOTHERHOOD

Some people seem to have made a great deal of fuss about single women opting to have a child by artificial insemination from a sperm bank.

Most women have an urge by LIFE to have children, but some do not wish to become wives, neither legal or common-law. So, what are they to do? Casual sex can lead to A.I.D.S. and V.D. and other sexual diseases. If they borrow their friends' husbands they could be highly unpopular. The sperm bank is supposed to offer sperm from healthy young males with the colour of hair, eyes and skin, classified so that the prospective mother can have some choice, as she may wish the child to have some resemblance to the other members of her family.

Of course, children do really need two parents, but with the present divorce rates, a great many have only one. Also there are all those women whose husbands have deserted them and all the single women whose partners did not want to know when they got pregnant and just left them.

The child in the future may resent never having known his own father, but as all children seem at some time to fantasize about their actual parents not being their real parents, and usually their fantasy parents are higher up the social scale or more important etc. the fantasy never need to come down to earth. The child will not suffer the trauma of divorced parents and custody battles and being sent like a parcel from one parent to the other.

The single women who are opting to become mothers are usually well enough off to provide for their children unlike many of the unfortunate single mothers who have been deserted.

It is only fairly recently that illegitimate children have been treated like any other children, if their illegitimacy was known about. At one time not so long ago, being a bastard (except in aristocratic circles) was a stigma for the rest of the person's life, and unmarried mothers were outcasts. The unmarried fathers were of course never blamed, just like today. Even if the woman was raped or drugged, it was still all her fault if she became pregnant, and many a poor girl committed suicide if her family would not stand by her. Abortion was illegal but "back street" abortions were common for those who knew where to go, but they often resulted in the death of the woman, or at least in her not being able to have any more children.

CHAPTER XII

SURROGATE MOTHERHOOD AND GENETIC ENGINEERING: WHERE WILL IT END?

Many women, desperate for a child, and unable to conceive, perhaps because of damaged fallopian tubes, are being helped by new methods.

Some years ago the first baby was born who was conceived *in vitro*, that is, in a glass dish. The ova (egg) had been extracted from the potential mother, a small operation but not without some risk, and sperm from the potential father fertilised the eggs. When the embryo had developed in the dish to a certain stage it was implanted in the woman's uterus, and nine month's later a healthy baby was born, if they were lucky. The rate of success is not yet very high.

We have seen on T.V. twins who were born years apart, the one embryo having been frozen. We have also seen on T.V. a grandmother giving birth to her triplet grandchildren by caesarian section. The *in vitro* fertilised *ova* were from her daughter and her daughter's husband, and then implanted in the daughter's mother's uterus because the daughter could not carry a child to term. A grandmother in South Dakota was having twins for her daughter who was born without a womb.

These experiments had been tried first with animals but without bothering about whether the sheep or cows were the actual parents. They were just surrogate wombs to what the animal owners thought were offspring of the best of the breed.

When the surgeon performs the operation on a woman, more than one egg is taken, so that if the first implant does not grow, another fertilised embryo can be implanted to try again. This means that many fertilised embryos may be left, and controversy reigns over whether these should be used for medical experiments or even for infertile couples to enable them to have a child which is not genetically theirs, but is a form of adoption in the womb.

But now that cells from aborted foetuses have been used as implants in the brains of some patients with Parkinson's disease, with so far, good results, another argument has broken out about the ethics of using these cells, previous use not having been noticed apparently. Surely the foetuses can be put to some good use instead of being destroyed?

It is said that human life is sacrosanct and so no experiments should be done on humans or potential humans. In actual fact only the lives of the powerful are sacrosanct.

The common people have been killed in their millions in wars waged by the powerful. Millions of them have been left to starve without any thought at all being given to them. And further millions have been deliberately starved by certain dictators. We can never know how many have been assassinated at various times. We do know of millions killed in Germany's gas chambers during World War II. But the exact toll we shall never know. We do not know how many die because of avoidable industrial conditions such as diseases of the lung caused by inhaling coal dusts etc, cancers caused by asbestos, by nitrites in the soil from artificial fertilisers etc. Or how many die in famines, volcanic eruptions, earthquakes and floods. How many people have been used as guinea pigs in hospitals for treatments given without their knowledge or consent?

One question about using these left-over embryos has been when does life begin? This is easily answered. It does not begin, it is already there. The egg is living and the sperm is living, so the fertilised egg is living. When does the embryo become a potential human being? One answer given is after fourteen days when apparently the nervous system starts to form. So, laboratories have been given the go-ahead for their experiments up to fourteen days after fertilisation. Then what happens to the foetuses? Some suggestions have been made. But how should we dispose of the rest?

Another question that needs an answer is, who should decide about the priority given to *in vitro* fertilisation instead of the money being given to improve the peri-natal conditions for the babies of the poorer members of our society, where thousands more wanted babies die, than in better off families.

GENETIC ENGINEERING

Genetic engineers can now (1990) divide up the developing egg after it has itself divided into four cells, to produce four identical offspring. These cells from a sheep were implanted into four different ewes to produce quads. In one case, one embryo from a cow was implanted in another cow, and the others frozen, so that when the resultant calf was of an age to reproduce, one of the frozen embryos developed from the quartering of the original egg, could be implanted and the calf (now cow) could give birth to its twin sister, or itself? I do not know if this has actually happened but it is possible. The mind boggles at the implications for the human race in the future. Because things can be done, they will be done, by somebody, somewhere.

There should be a world-wide ban on patenting human genes, because they are discoveries and not inventions. Nobody has yet made a new gene.

Genentech the U.S. based biotechnology firm has taken out a licence to patent relaxin with a view to marketing the human version as an obstetric drug. Relaxin is a hormone that causes the muscles of the birth canal to relax and is produced by the ovaries during labour. Doctors have now discovered a way to generate human bone marrow from cells found in the umbilical cords of new-born babies. Once again this is a discovery but it has been patented in the U.S. It is to be used for leukaemia victims who previously had to wait for a volunteer donor to allow bone marrow to be extracted from, usually, their spinal column. The cords were previously thrown away.

OTHER GENETIC ENGINEERING

Genetic engineers have produced insulin implants from donors which will enable the diabetic patient's pancreas to produce its own insulin, they hope. They are also hoping to remove the defective genes which cause inherited diseases like cystic fibrosis, Huntingdon's chorea etc. Among other gene implants there are now sheep with gene implants that cause the wool in their coats to break at a certain time so that they need no longer be sheared. The fleece can be pulled off. This has lead to many sheep suffering very badly from sunburn because they have no hair on their bodies. Previously many used to die of infected cuts after shearing and of course from pneumonia if the weather turned cold, which of course they will still do.

SURROGATE MOTHERHOOD

These fertilised egg implants mean that no woman who does not wish, and who has enough money to pay, need actually have her own child. She can rent a womb. It is already happening in America and although it is frowned on here (and may become illegal) it is actually happening here that women are being paid to have a nine-month's pregnancy and to give birth to another woman's child.

There have already been some set-backs with the surrogate mothers refusing to give up the child they have borne although they have agreed that the child is not actually theirs.

These must be mothers with a strong maternal instinct. It is thought that a woman's maternal feelings will not be aroused for a child she has not carried to term and brought to birth. But this maternal instinct does not work for some women. I have known women who have longed for a child, and then been bitterly disappointed when they felt nothing for the child after giving it birth. For them love for the child, if it happens at all, comes from looking after it and watching it grow. Some women never feel this love, and their's are the unfortunate children who get neglected and abused. Some mothers are known to actually hate their children, perhaps because they are too like their husbands from whom they have parted, or even because they are ugly or deformed, physically or mentally. They are ashamed of having produced them.

Kissing goes by favour. How can we tell why some are loved and others are not?

There may be legal difficulties with the children of surrogate mothers about inheritance and proof of origin of the children. That is for the lawyers to sort out and get richer. Career women will be able to continue with their careers without interruption if they so wish, and rich women will be able to continue their social whirl and retain their figures. I am sure that Queen Victoria would have been one of the first to employ a surrogate mother if it had been possible in her day. She did so hate having children and she had nine. Remember, she was the first to use chloroform for a birth, and made it acceptable for all women who could pay for it.

The well-off had always employed "wet-nurses" that is, women who had just had a child, and who had plenty of breast-milk. There were no baby foods on the market so breast-milk was essential if the child was to live. It was life itself to the child. Some "wet-nurses" were so poverty stricken that they would leave their new-born baby to someone else to feed, just to get money to feed their other children, and would even agree not to see their own children until the child of the employer was weaned. Charles Dickens wrote of this practice in *Dombey and son*. When Dombey's wife died, he employed a "wet-nurse" on these terms. Dickens knew well what the poor of his time had to put up with.

Now, of course, any woman who does not wish, or is not able to breast-feed her baby, can bottle feed it with one of the many baby food formulas. We are told by doctors that breast-fed babies are immune against diseases and also that they may have a higher I.Q. than babies fed on formulas.

The baby food manufacturers have turned their attention to the Third world for a new market. This has lead to a lot of children in the poorer countries dying of malnutrition when the baby food manufacturers have by advertisements, persuaded mothers that their product is better than the mother's own milk. The mothers have been unable to buy quantities sufficient to nourish the babies and they have died.

CHAPTER XIII

TELEVISION: MAKES THE WHOLE WORLD LOOK ALIKE?

Television has been and still is, a great boon to many people. It could be the greatest educator the world has ever known.

Our ancestors would have thought of it as a miracle something talked about in fairy tales but not something that everyone could have. But just like us they would have soon taken it for granted.

I remember when T.V. was first broadcast just after the Second World War, (only London had T.V. in 1936 and that was discontinued for the duration of the war.) We had a little nine-inch screen with pictures in black and white, and people said as a joke, "I am not having T.V. until the picture is three times as big and in colour." This is no longer a joke. Everybody can have the minor miracle.

At first, people with pretensions to be superior thought it was only suitable for the lower classes. Writers and actors and actresses were all very wary of working for T.V. as they thought it lowered their status. Now they are all eager to appear even on the commercials that accompany the programmes. It is more lucrative than anything else they do, except appearing in films, and they get more publicity.

There are still a few eccentrics who refuse to have a T.V. set in the house, usually because they say the children are better without it. Of course the children do not know what the other children at school are talking about, and to them, watching a friend's T.V. set is a special treat, which is not what their parents intend at all! These parents usually permit radio sets in their homes. Radio has been around long enough to be acceptable.

Television is the greatest boon to those people who live alone. They are often elderly with very few friends left in the world. The characters they see on T.V. especially the ones in the soap operas that they follow, seem to some of them, like personal friends. They write to them and send them presents just as if the shadows they see are more lifelike to them than the people they actually know. These are the sort of people, who, when they went to the theatre in the days before T.V. used to tell the hero when the villain was coming, and if they met the actor who portrayed the villain on the street, they would revile him for his dastardly deeds. They still confuse reality with fantasy.

There are those who think that everything, including the news is something cooked up in the studio. They may, sometimes be right to be so cynical. These folk think that nobody went into space or landed on the moon. It was all done by the effects department. After all they had seen more spectacular shows on T.V. done with camera trickery, and they had been deceived so often that no wonder they were sceptical about the whole space programme.

T.V. can be used equally to educate us and to deceive us. In some countries T.V. is controlled by the State so that their populations only see what their Governments will allow them to see. We pride ourselves that the B.B.C. is independent and can show us the truth. But during the Falklands dispute, the Government took over, and what did we see? Of course it was all in the name of security.

There have been some wonderful series on T.V. about the natural world. We have seen splendidly photographed programmes about animals, plants, fish, insects, etc., that few of us would have been fortunate enough to see in a couple of life-times (if we had them.)

The Chinese are reputed to have said that a picture is worth a thousand words, and the pictures have certainly brought home to us what a struggle for life goes on everywhere, every plant struggling against all the others for space, water and nutrients, and every animal looking over its shoulder (of it has one) for the plant, insect or animal that wants it for dinner. The countryside and gardens that look so peaceful to us are a lethal battleground for a myriad of plants and creatures. We can also see how we are crowding Life's wonderful creations off the face of the Earth. We have all seen it. We all know. We no longer have the excuse that we did not know what we were doing. Once they go they are gone for ever. We cannot re-create them.

It is said by some that T.V. has killed conversation. I ask what conversation? People who like talking will go on talking, nothing will stop them. The rest of us mostly gossip (and nothing can kill that off I am glad to say) or bore everybody to death with our pet themes.

All sport fanatics have had a bonanza. All the highlights without having to endure the boring bits. Also, more people have probably taken up sport since seeing so many varieties, but I doubt if it is very good for one's ego to see the best in the world and compare it with one's own efforts. T.V. programmers try to find something for every taste. Long live the mishmash. We all have an off button.

When grumbling about the things they do not like on television viewers seem to lump sex and violence together. Why? The one should be the opposite of the other. A great deal of entertainment is concerned with murder and killing even if it is disguised as detection and prevention, and very few people even raise a murmur of disapproval. But sex is often condemned. I must admit it is pretty boring watching other people perform, but I suppose it might be a "Turn on" for some people which is obviously what is intended. It is not supposed to be shown while children are still watching, but until they themselves reach puberty it usually means nothing to them, except for thinking that grown-ups are soppy and silly. But they are allowed to watch killing and maiming all day long. Violence on T.V. is blamed for crime and hooliganism. Before T.V. it was blamed on the cinema. What was it blamed on before that? There was probably even more violence in the days before either were available. But if T.V. has no influence on people why are the advertisers wasting their money?

Many people (mostly women) dislike hearing what used to be called "gutter language" on T.V. Bad language is either anatomical, lavatorial, or about sexual perversions or illegitimacy, and it does get very boring. It is a form of idleness using these few words, because it is so much easier than writing a good script. Because they listen, even very young children now use all the known swearwords most of the time. It used to be that only the children of parents who swore used this sort of language. The words no longer have any meaning for anyone.

Television, especially American television, which has been exported all over the world, has shown the poorer countries the comparatively rich lives of the Western world. Now they all want the goodies for themselves. It has also ensured that Western civilisation will prevail over most of the world, and all cities will look alike, with the same style of buildings, cars and chain stores etc., and with everybody wearing the same sort of clothes, and probably all speaking American English, which will become most countries' second language.

Television has had more influence on the world's populations than even the motor car, and the aeroplane, but it has not managed to make all the peoples of the Earth into on Global Nation which may be the only way that the Earth will be saved from destruction.

CHAPTER XIV

NEWSPAPERS AND RED HERRINGS

All the newspapers in this country are in the hands of the Conservatives and all the news is slanted towards the Tory right, being the right.

Tory Right wing views show a belief in: hierarchy, nationalism, censorship, elitist education, hereditary privilege and the desirability of revenge; and the concept of retribution in penal policy. Views which the Tories kept quiet about for many years after the War (according to Mr. Peregrine Worsthorne) for fear of being proscribed as Fascists.

The Home Office has protected in the past, the Fascist Organisation calling itself the National Front, by shepherding its members with hordes of police during its organised marches through districts inhabitated by the poor and the coloured people. The Home Office could have banned the marches, but it preferred to protect the Fascists. The Second World War was supposed to have been a war against Fascism.

We do not know who chooses what shall be published as news. We do know if we happened to have been present at some scenes described, that they were vastly different from the accounts published.

We know that a restriction can be put on anything the Government of the time does not want published, and prison sentences and possible loss of a career can be meted out to anyone leaking so-called confidential material, even if it is something that commonsense says that everybody has a right to know as it vitally concerns them.

RED HERRINGS

Instead of debating issues that are of importance to everyone, newspapers often resort to red herrings, any little topic that will turn people's attention from what really matters. Once such topic was the non-return of supermarket trolleys. Everybody got duly incensed about the problem although it was really something for the supermarkets themselves to deal with, which is what some of them have now done.

DOGS

Another item is the perpetual anti-dog report. At first dogs were supposed to be causing eye trouble with children who chose to play in dog mess. Then they were supposed to be causing the streets to be filthy with dog turds. Dog turds wash away in the rain, but all the broken glass, beer cans, plastic wrappings, and fish and chip wrappers are ankle deep in many streets, and dogs are not responsible for that sort of permanent rubbish. It strikes me that all the people who used to rush out with a shovel and a bucket whenever a horse approached, might well do the same with dog turds. They are probably good cheap fertiliser.

At one time, dog turds were used in tanning all sorts of leather, and the fortunes of some now-called top people were founded on shipping dog excrement from other countries; but of course they would be reluctant now to admit it. Perhaps some enterprising entrepreneur will make a fortune by selling it as fertiliser, or even to add a disagreeable smell to glue solvents to prevent what I am told is an epidemic of glue sniffing among the young.

I think we should remember what the Belgian philosopher, Maurice Maeterlinck, wrote about dogs:

> "We are alone, absolutely alone on this chance planet, and amid all the forms of life that surrounds us, not one, excepting the dog, has made an alliance with us. Not only is the dog man's best friend, he is man's only friend, and his loyalty is greater than man's."

HOOLIGANISM

Hooliganism like the poor, has always been with us, and is not likely to go away. If it is hooliganism by the so-called upperclasses it is "high spirits" and father pays for the damage. It has been endlessly discussed on T.V. and in newspapers, and Parliament devoted hours of debate to the subject. All this to take people's minds off subjects that really matter to them, like the unfair poll-tax, and the selling off, to a few people and a lot of companies, the property which they already owned such as the Gas, Electricity and Water industries, all of which was illegal because it was not the Government which owned them, but the nation as a whole. They were encouraged by the TSB bank being allowed by an English judge to sell off what they did not own, after a Scottish judge had ruled that it was not legal.

As hooliganism seems to be a facet of young manhood in other countries as well as in the U.K.; a place should be found where it could be controlled while the youths got the aggression out of their systems without inconveniencing anyone else. Fist only punch-ups could be arranged in different parts of the country every week-end (no bottles or weapons) so that real football fans could watch the game in peace, and we could give up debating the subject.

The "upper classes" send their young men into the Guards but the Army would not welcome other nuisances except of course in time of war.

CHAPTER XV

ART, PAINTING, SCULPTURE: MY PREJUDICES

All painting is fantasy whether it is a portrait or a view or an abstract. It is a two dimensional representation as seen or imagined by one person. Much as I love fine paintings I cannot believe that a two dimensional representation of a living being is worth more than the actual being.

Paintings today are judged by their marketable value, that is, by how much anyone is prepared to pay for a signature. If the painting is proved to be by someone other than the illustrious name, its value drops to next to nothing although the actual picture has not changed. And who decides the market value? The firms that sell the paintings. They put a big reserve price on paintings and if they are not sold they are "bought in" by a pretend buyer. They get a percentage both on buying and selling the paintings and *objets d'art* so the more they can persuade anyone to pay the better off they are. This has a knock-on effect on future sales.

I do not know if the 36 or so paintings attributed to Vermeer are signed. I rather think they may not be, as they have been previously assigned to other artists. There is one *The Head of a Girl* in a museum in Amsterdam, which I think is not by him at all. I think it is a self-portrait by an unknown artist. Wouldn't its value drop if I was proved to be right? What sort of art appreciation is this?

Photography has taken the place of oil painting in one of its previous functions; to let the world know how rich you were, how you could afford fine jewels and fine clothes and had vast estates.

With modern travel you do not even have to send your portrait, to your intended or whatever, you can just pop over, or alternatively, send a few inexpensive photographs. Just think how Henry VIII would have liked that before he married Anne of Cleves. So, with the advent of photography a lot of painters thought that representational art was finished, and the only way forward was grotesque or abstract painting. Future generations will think we were mad to even bother to look at such boring pictures; but really very few people do bother. Most of the population just ignore them. It is only the "experts" who value them and persuade those with lots of money to buy them as investments.

This is the first age when an artist is so-called when he can neither draw nor paint. The Art prizes go to those who seem to throw paint about in large quantities with no method in their madness.

If you look at the reproductions that people actually put up on their walls, or at the affordable originals they buy, you will see that representational painting is still very much alive. A painting has a liveliness that is missing from most photographs if it is skilled enough.

ARCHITECTURE

It is a pity that the skyscraper was ever invented and built. It is said that it originated in New York because there was no room to spread out. It has made every city in the world look like a collection of upturned cigar boxes, all as dead boring as one another.

As homes for ordinary people, they are highly unpopular,

expensive to maintain, and a target for vandals. In some cities tower blocks for the poor have had to be taken down. Folk do not like living in up-ended streets with no contact with the Earth. If on the other hand they are refurbished for the rich and in more desirable environments, complete with caretakers and security guards, lifts that work, and surrounded by greenery, they can become quite acceptable, especially if they are in Monaco.

Most of today's buildings seem to be of concrete. Can there be anything more dismal looking than concrete? There are a few new good buildings around. I gather that the new museum outside Glasgow to house the Burrell collection is one such pleasing edifice.

In future ages (if any) this will be known as the TRASH age. The buildings are mostly trash compared with those erected centuries go. It is the same with music, the more rubbishy it sounds the more it is acclaimed. There are even very few popular songs written that can be whistled. The pop singers write their own trash and they all sound alike, the noisier the better, with little singing, just screaming and shouting.

Fashion today is just trash. The fashion shows are just fancy dress. The girls walking in the streets wear Doc Marten's boots with flimsy long summer dresses or ragged jeans and white so-called trainers; oversized blouses or shirts with oversize anoraks and sporting hair like hay. The boys wear the same ragged jeans and multi-coloured anoraks and with either shaved heads or long, dank hair. The amusing grotesque hair styles have now gone out, but they will be back. Sculpture too is mostly trash, just lumps of stone with holes here and there.

I daresay that there are many people to-day who could achieve what the artists and sculptors of ancient times achieved in every field, but who wants that sort of perfection in the age of TRASH?

The only ones who want perfection are the ones who can afford antiques, the older the more esteemed. This has led to many forgeries of paintings of so-called old masters. Some forgers have been detected and some even sent to jail, but usually the only people who have really benefited from the forgeries have been the dealers and none of them to my knowledge have ended up in jail. There are reputed to be forgeries in all the major art galleries of the world.

The value that man puts on all his works must be very little indeed, judging by the enthusiasm with which he smashes everything in the constant wars he wages. I mean *man* here, when I say *man*; women seem to have little say in waging these wars.

CHAPTER XVI

COMPUTERS: WHERE DO WE GO FROM HERE?

Computers will shortly rule most of our lives. The silicon chip and gallium arsenide and whatever is next in the pipeline have made computers so small and so cheap that they can be used to organize most jobs out of existence. The only jobs likely to be left are the service jobs such as doctors (although their diagnostic skills may be superseded by computers) dentists, nurses, mothers and housewives and computer programming. I see no sign yet of housekeeping and housework being computerised out of existence.

Writing poetry, stories and scripts will still need human imagination, but these activities have been poorly paid, except for a few, so not many manage to keep their families or get rich doing it.

Computer programmers are trying to put the translators out of work. I suppose computers could translate English if it was free from gobbledy-gook, ambiguities, idioms, and slang and if the words had only one meaning instead of a meaning in the context of the sentence. Imagine a computer realising the difference between "you have it" meaning exactly that and "you have had it" meaning that you are not likely to get it, and "you have had it" meaning you have had enough and are finished. One much quoted example is: "Out of sight, out of mind." Translation: "Invisible idiot".

Computers and the consequent automation means that many people will not be able to get work to support themselves and their families. What sort of life are they going to lead as the rich get richer and the poor get poorer? One thing is for sure, the rich do not want to know about the poor. They will just ignore them and their miseries just as they have always done. The poor themselves are so busy being jealous of other poor people who are slightly better off than they are themselves that they have no time or energy left to be envious of the rich, yet.

It will be up to a concerned Government, concerned about the welfare of the poor, and concerned that it is not sowing the seeds of revolution, to ensure that, out of the vast profits made by the use of computers, sufficient is made over to the unwaged to keep them reasonably content.

CHAPTER XVII

CRIME

Every age and every country has had a different idea of which are the worst crimes against society.

In the United Kingdom crime against property has always been rated higher than crimes against the person, especially if that person is poor or is a woman.

The "great train robbers" were given thirty years in jail, while many a man has been out of prison in 18 months after murdering his wife or another woman if he pleads provocation. One man was given a suspended sentence because he said his wife nagged him. Almost at the same time a woman was given a life sentence when she murdered her husband after years of being beaten up by her drunken husband.

Provocation for a man can be anything from telling him that he is not the world's greatest lover, to telling him that the woman wants to be left alone. In one case a man said that he strangled his wife in a dream because he dreamt that she was unfaithful. He too got a light sentence.

The criminal Damages Bill of 1982 suggested an award of damages to a woman £2,700 for rape, and £7,000 for a scar on man's face. Even in child abuse cases, there is a great difference in the Court's attitude to abuse of little girls and little boys. 85% of child abuse is of little girls but abusers of girls receive a sentence on average of five years, while for abusers for boys it is ten years.

CARNAGE ON THE ROADS

The carnage on the roads is mostly ignored except by the relatives of the people killed and injured. Thousands of people are killed every year and thousands more injured. Drunken driving and speed are two of the main causes of this great loss of life and loss of mobility, but nothing much is done about it.

A new breathalyser is brought in now and again but ways are found of outwitting the evidence and drunken driving goes on. The tax collected from alcohol means that the Government of the day will not move against the Brewery lobby, and allow breath tests outside public houses where the drunks start their driving.

Those who cause death by drunken driving often get off with a small fine. They should at least be charged with man slaughter.

Despite the evidence from America that fewer people have been killed on the roads since a 55 mile an hour limit has been enforced, there are people in Britain who advocate putting the 70 mile an hour limit up to 80 miles per hour because so many people break the law already and drive even faster. The same people would still break the law and drive even faster. Since when has breaking the law been any excuse for rescinding the law? Should we make burglary lawful because of the number of people who break the law?

In future times (if any) people will think we were quite mad to allow more people to be killed or maimed on the roads than were ever killed in all the wars throughout history.

If an epidemic broke out (of any disease) and it killed and maimed all the occupants of a small town, the same number who are killed or maimed on our roads every year, everybody would be very frightened and demand that somebody should so something about it. But because nobody wants to restrict personalised transport in any way, we all shut our eyes to the carnage.

At the same time we can get very emotional when a few people are killed in a train smash, or a plane crash or even if one person is killed by a bomb. We humans are very peculiar, we only see the disasters we want to see.

We could have cars fixed so that they could not exceed the speed limit. We could give everybody six months without the option for drunken driving. We could confiscate their cars. Of course many of the cars on the road are company cars but even they might get tired of having their cars confiscated. Of course I realise that car manufacturers would block anything that would lead to cars not being sold with the macho image they try to give them today. They are advertised as faster, ever faster. Just look at the names they give them. To many a man, his car is the love of his life. He cherishes it more than he cherishes his wife. But as soon as a newer model becomes accessible to him, it is off with the old love and on with the new, without a backward glance.

BURGLARY, ASSAULT AND THEFT

Most of the occupants of our overcrowded prisons have been convicted of (or are on remand) for either or all of these crimes. They are mostly crimes against the poor. Thousands more get away with these crimes than are ever caught. But of those who are caught, many will spend many years in prison for stealing relatively small sums. They are usually inadequate men who have no thought for the misery they cause. Others prefer to steal instead of working, as the likelihood of getting caught is slim. Why don't they rob the rich who are insured and can afford to lose things? Usually because the rich have better security, and the search by the police to detect the criminal is more sustained. The Government's "law and order" policies are mainly about these crimes. That is, mainly directed towards the poor.

DRUGS

All the police forces of the world are fighting a losing battle against the "Drug Barons" the distributers and the drug "pushers." It reminds me of "Prohibition" in the United States which led to greater evils than alcoholism, murders, bootlegging of spirits that blinded people, and gangsters who seemed to control whole cities. The Act was eventually repealed as being impossible to enforce.

But some American States are still "dry" today. I suppose people can choose where they wish to live and move to another State if they wish to consume alcohol.

Eventually drugs will have to be legalised, just as tobacco and alcohol are legalised, because there is no way of stopping their use.

Cannabis should certainly be legalised. It was only prohibited in the first place because it made workers dopey and they did not work so hard.

I have not heard of anyone killing any other person while using it, which is more than you say about alcohol. I have never felt the urge to try it myself so I can say nothing from first-hand experience about its effects.

If all drugs are legalised the price should drop which should lead to less thieving by users to get the money to buy it. And the "Drug Barons" will still get rich, but not so easily. Of course they could restrict the supply to keep the prices up. If they are legalised, the so-called "hard drugs" should carry a dire warning such as:

"If you try this once, it may kill you. It has killed many others. If it does not kill you immediately you could find yourself hooked on it and unable to live without it. Your whole life will revolve around it and become worthless. Very few people have been able to kick the habit. You may not be one of them." Legalising drugs should leave the Police free to combat other crimes.

WORSE CRIMES

The bigger crimes against people in general carry little or no punishment. Crimes such as polluting the atmosphere, the Earth, the water etc. Because it would reduce their profits polluters are mainly allowed to get away with it. Government reports on pollution are secret, so it is extremely difficult and costly for anyone to bring an action for damages against polluters and moreover the action is likely to fail because he companies are so powerful. Profits come before the health of the people who are endangered by all this pollution.

Tax avoidance and evasion is a crime against society in as much as it leaves the burden of financing the State on other people, and mainly on the shoulders of those who pay on PAYE and who have no say in how their money should be spent.

Other people I regard as criminals are those who make large

profits for themselves from the work of those to whom they pay as little as they can get away with.

Manufacturing and selling armaments all over the world can be nothing but a crime against humanity. Some people think that the First World War was partly caused by the armament manufacturers. Many smaller wars have been encouraged to happen by the Military sections of the Government wishing to test their armaments.

I regard as arch criminals everywhere, those who devise yet more horrible ways of destroying people, including chemical and bacterial weapons. Of course these people would say it is a job and they are only obeying orders like all the other atrocity committers.

We have all heard of the big criminals such as Attila the Hun, Caligula the Roman Emperor, Vladimir the Impaler, and in modern times Adolf Hitler, the German meglomaniac who so nearly conquered the whole of Europe, and was only foiled in the first place because he chose to invade Russia and Russia defeated him.

He was the cause of millions of deaths and atrocities (remember the concentration camps and the gas ovens?) but who was behind him? Who provided the money and the power? Most school children today do not seem to have even heard of Hitler let alone what he did. I can understand this in Germany where they naturally wish to forget their past, but not in the rest of the world. Stalin, the Russian Dictator (in effect but not in name) who caused millions of people to be killed in his "purges" and let millions more starve to death, and the dictators of smaller so-called Republics, where thousands of people disappear and are never seen again, these are the real criminals. We must not forget those who commit atrocities because they say they are obeying orders. They are just as evil as those who give the orders.

Then there are the rapists, murderers of children and old people; those who murder anyone who get in their way and feel no remorse because they just like torturing and killing. These people have a field day during a war when nobody knows who is killing who.

Humans are the only species who will torture their own kind. I can only think that humans are the cruellest animals in the world, both to their own kind and every living thing on this Earth.

CHAPTER XVIII

WAR, MASS MURDER: WILL IT EVER STOP?

Making war on his fellow humans seems to be one of the programmes that LIFE has given to men, so I doubt if they ever can change.

If the Government of the day instigates it and approves of it is called war, and so it is honourable no matter how many lives are lost and how horrible all the killing and maiming is. If a group of people without the sanction of the Government kill people in the same way it is called mass murder and everyone is horrified.

No other species except man kills his own species in large numbers. Other animals fight for territories to have enough food for themselves and their families, and they fight for females, but very few fight to the death. Man fights because he likes to fight and destroy everything regardless of the consequences. Peaceful life is too dull for him. So wars will continue everywhere. Often men do not know what they are fighting about.

We very rarely hear the opinion of women during these wars; as they are programmed to be the creators I cannot believe that they are also programmed to be the destroyers. They stand to lose the most in these conflicts. Perhaps not all men are programmed for war on humans. It has been reported that 60,000 American soldiers who fought in the Vietnam war have committed suicide.

NUCLEAR WAR

So far no-one has dared to start a nuclear war, but now that so many truly catastrophic weapons have been stockpiled all over the world and so many countries now have nuclear bombs, it is inevitable that one day they will be used.

However, once a nuclear war starts there will be no way of stopping it even if it starts by accident, by some malfunction of somebody's brain or a malfunction of a computer or other machine, or even by a smaller country that cannot win by any other means. But you cannot win a war by destroying the world. Every country has missiles trained on the seat of authority in other countries, so there will be no means of ending the holocaust once it has started. There are estimated to be over 40,000 nuclear warheads in the world today.

Some American statesmen seem to imagine that there can be a nuclear war in Europe that will not affect them. Their one-time defence minister said on television that as the last two wars had been mainly fought in Europe, he saw no reason why the next war should not be confined to Europe. President John F. Kennedy brought us very near to a nuclear war at the Bay of Pigs and former Presidential candidate Gary Hart has revealed on Irish T.V's "Late late" show, that an accidental nuclear war between the Soviet Union and the U.S. ten years ago was narrowly averted. He said that the American Early Warning system developed a major fault. Radar screens showed a huge fleet of Soviet missiles approaching the U.S.A. All the American defence systems were put on the alert and only at the last minute before President Ronald Reagan was to have given the signal to activate them was it realised that the soviet missiles were just the result of a malfunction of the Early Warning system. It only needs another malfunction somewhere that is not rectified at the last minute, and it may be the end for most of us.

SURVIVORS OF A NUCLEAR WAR

If a nuclear war destroys most of the world, everybody may not vanish. Some groups of rich people with well-stocked hide-outs in the mountains may survive (if they happen to be in their hide-out when doom day happens.) They may learn to live without modern technical miracles. Some Government officials may survive if they manage to reach their underground sanctuaries in time. The Chinese, being a quarter of the Earth's population may have some survivors from their 800 million farmers who mostly farm in the same way as their ancestors have always farmed without the technical help that the farmers of the West enjoy.

Not many people in Britain would survive. As the Americans said in the second World War "Great Britain is a small group of islands off the coast of Europe. They are expendable." And so they will be. Target Number one when the bombs start falling.

Scientists tell us that even a limited (?) nuclear war would cause great clouds of dust which would blot out the light and the heat of the sun for many months so that most of the vegetation would die. So, unless the survivors had great stocks of food and water they could die of starvation if they did not die of radiation.

H.G. Wells, the father of science fiction writing (yes I do remember Jules Verne) prophesied in his book *The Shape of Things to Come* published in 1934, just when the second world war would start, (he was one year out) and the actual place where it would start, Danzig in Poland now Gdansk, and also that no peace treaty would be signed, which is also true. And that after the third world war there would be only small groups of wanderers inhabitating the Earth. This again could well be true.

I do not believe in crystal balls and those who profess to tell the future, because they could become the richest people on Earth if they could only tell which horse would win, or how the stock market would move, but I do wonder how H.G. Wells could prophecy world events so accurately.

Mankind has always been motivated by fear and greed, not love and sweet reasonableness and common sense as we like to delude ourselves. Just fear and greed plus envy. If fear of a nuclear holocaust cannot save the world, perhaps greed will. I am referring to the great international companies who wield great power and of course make great profits. They build their factories where labour is cheap. The have built their factories in Communist countries where strikes were forbidden and the Government kept the wages down so making more profits for the multi-nationals. So the Western world profited at the expense of the Communist world. What happens now that communism is out of fashion? Nuclear war would destroy the multinationals factories and their markets along with everything else. The multi-nationals might have the power to prevent world catastrophe where nobody wins.

Are you prepared to risk a holocaust? Remember it is your world just as much as anyone else's. You have as much right to the Earth as any other living being. No-one can compel you to assist in the destruction of the Earth. If you say that you are just obeying orders (which nobody has the right to give) then you are just as insane as the people giving the orders and there is no hope for anyone. Read the book *The Fate of the Earth* by Jonathan Schell. Remember the graffiti "All men were cremated equal."

TINDER BOXES AND ICE-AGES

Of course there are other ways of finishing off the human race and the Earth. Professor J.E. Lovelock, one of the world's leading authorities on atmospheric chemistry, predicts that an increase of only 1% in the proportion of oxygen in the atmosphere would turn the Earth into a tinder-box and everything would go up in flames. Nobody, but nobody really knows how the balance between oxygen removed and oxygen added to our atmosphere is achieved. And nobody really knows how the belts round our atmosphere prevent it from leaking into space.

It may be that nuclear missiles exploded in the stratosphere may damage these belts and the air will leak out, and then exit all organisms that require oxygen to live and only the bacteria that live in the gases of volcanoes will once again be the world's only inhabitants.

Professor Fred Hoyle is predicting a new ice-age lasting for 50,000 years unless we do something about it. Ice-ages have predominated over the Earth's climate with only shorter warmer periods for millions of years so of course he could be right.

It may be that Nature (LIFE) has decided that mankind was all a great mistake, and so has allowed men to discover a way to eliminate most of the human race.

Life has been starting all over again and again for the millions of years the Earth has been in space. But if LIFE came to Earth from other worlds it does seem to need some vehicle to get to yet other worlds (meteorites or perhaps spaceships) so perhaps we shall be prevented from eliminating ourselves until we have sent a lot more and better spaceships hurtling into space. A certain Mr. Cobb wrote an epitaph for the people of the Earth:

"A belated advertisement for a line of goods that has been permanently discontinued."

CHAPTER XIX

PORNOGRAPHY: WHO NEEDS IT?

Paintings and sculptures of female nudes have adorned the bedrooms of the wealthy since art began. Pornography for the rich? In one of the houses in the ruins of Pompeii all the pictures of sexual intercourse taking place have all been gathered into one room, the Italians being unlike the Indians where such displays adorn every temple.

The Greeks and the Romans used to depict their male statues completely nude (The statue of *David* in Florence, is perhaps a copy?) Whereas Victorian Englishmen mostly chose to cover male genitalia with large fig leaves (Fig leaves from presumably the references in the Bible). Even in Art schools in my time, the female models were quite nude (but with their pubic hair removed) while the males wore minute trunks. Most Victorian women, unless they came from large families living in cramped conditions probably had never seen a male nude until they married one. (That may still be true today if a girl is the only child!)

Today offices and work places are plastered with pictures of naked women, but if any woman working there puts up a picture of a naked man it is immediately torn down. If she objects to the naked women photographs she is told she can't take a joke. Why should she when she is the joke?

Pornography is about women, not men. Men are not coy in the showers after playing games, so why are they so shy about displaying their sexual equipment? After all, most women have to get used to male genitals if they marry or have relationships. Are the men afraid of comparisons? Afraid that women will laugh at them in the same way they laugh at women? I am not advocating that men go about exposing themselves except on nude beaches and islands, any more than I am advocating that women should be so exposed. But what is sauce for the goose. The old men who deliberately expose themselves to young girls are usually a pretty revolting sight for anyone to see. Usually poor things they are mentally or physically afflicted.

The so-called "girlie mags" on sale in every newsagent are known as "soft porn". Nevertheless they are mostly an insult to women. Real women wonder what is wrong with them that their husbands delight so in these magazines. I think all these sort of pictures of women as just men's playthings have done great harm to women. These and all the advertisements have lead to these silly slimming crazes for women. Most men do not seem to bother what they look like with their beer bellies. When people are starving in the world slimming crazes seem obscene.

Real pornography is that depicting the humiliation and mutilation of women in all sorts of horrible ways by men. Is this real hatred or are they really so frightened of women? These "nasties" are available to anyone. Even if the law gets around to forbidding their sale, they will always be available on the black market.

Why do men hate women? A woman gave them birth and looked after them in their long childhood. A woman gave them life, and some repay with hatred and even death.

Comedy as portrayed on T.V. (and before that in Music Halls) is mostly jokes about sex, and men and women's anatomy. Most of the 51% of the population, who are women fail to see anything funny in the anatomy jokes, especially the ones about women's anatomy. They rightly feel embarrassed. Being denigrated is no joke, especially on T.V. with the family watching.

The other jokes are mainly lavatory jokes, and the men who find these funny are usually too squeamish to change the baby's nappies let alone wash them. Perhaps if they had to do a regular bed-pan round in a hospital they might not find human excrement so funny.

We have heard a lot lately about prisoners in out-of-date prisons having to "slop out" that is empty their chamber pots or pails. Of course it is revolting that these conditions continue, but women have been expected to do that service for their whole families for centuries. And many still do because there are still houses with only outside toilets. Let us make things better for the women who have not committed any crimes before we spend money on criminals. But of course they are only women, and women do not count do they? I wonder if prisoners from out-of-date jails still find lavatory jokes funny?

Men's obsession with the female breast seems to stop when the breast is being used for the function for which it was designed by LIFE. We see photographs of breasts in the newspapers "topless" women and nude women on beaches everywhere and of course on countless calendars, but if a woman starts to feed her hungry baby in public there is an outcry. In Restaurants, she is told, usually none too politely to retire to the toilets to feed her young. Why should not the infant be fed at the same dining table as he will be when he get a bit older?

In my young days, there were no "formulas" for feeding infants, so women breast-fed their babies when the said babies were hungry wherever they happened to be; in trains, waiting rooms, restaurants or wherever and nobody took any notice because it was not unusual. That is to say before the female breast became in male eyes an obsessional decorative bit of female anatomy. Somebody said, "female breasts are like train sets, meant for the children but played with by men." This may be why some men do not like their wives to breast-feed their babies although they know that it is much the best for the child, and much easier than preparing bottles, and as somebody said the cat can't get at the milk. It has been said that pornography "is for the poor souls who cannot get it up" (that is the sanitised version).

CHAPTER XX

DEATH AND LIFE: QUIT BROODING ABOUT DEATH, AND LIVE

Everything that lives is just a vehicle for LIFE and when something happens to that vehicle LIFE escapes and is presumably ready to enter a new vehicle. We do not know what LIFE is any more than we know what electricity is. We just know how it behaves. As darkness is the absence of light so is death the absence of LIFE self-evident.

Because LIFE escapes every time, it can arrange that one species can kill and eat any other species or even sometimes its own species. Every living thing except man is in the food chain. And sometimes, when driven to it by hunger, man eats man.

Cannibalism has happened in various parts of the world at different times. Sometimes men ate their enemies as food not to be wasted, and sometimes to acquire the qualities they admired in their enemies. Shipwrecked sailors have eaten one another. Explorers and pioneers have eaten people to survive. Survivors of a plane crash high in the Andes fairly recently, are said to have eaten the ones who died in the crash, when the food supplies ran out.

Human bodies when LIFE has left them, used to be returned to the earth to become nutrient for new life, but the fashion is now to cremate and return nothing to the Earth except a few meagre ashes. Space has become valuable and not to be wasted on cemeteries. In the same way, human waste used to help to fertilize the soil.

In Great Britain there was a Public Health Act forbidding the use of human waste as fertiliser, after various cholera outbreaks.

I do not know if that is still in force as at one time some sewage works sold a sanitized version for use as garden fertiliser. In China, I believe, human waste is still used on gardens and farms.

We must all live as if we think we are immortal. Death comes to us all eventually so there is no point in wasting your life brooding about it.

If we knew exactly when we would die, most of us would not be able to live our normal lives. Our minds would become unhinged and we would live like zombies, the walking dead. When we become very ill, some of us will have a presentiment that we will shortly die, but whether that is because we are losing the will to live, or because the body can no longer cope, we do not know.

All deaths except for wars and executions and epidemics are random, but there is usually an overall pattern so that insurance firms are able to predict, approximately, the number of each age group who will die in any one year.

ZOMBIES

Zombies, the walking dead in Haiti were usually poisoned (often by their relatives) with the highly poisonous toad Bufo Marinus or with the puffer fish. The most potent poison in the puffer fish is tetrodototoxin a deadly nerve poison. It causes paralysis and the victims are declared dead and then buried. Subsequently the poisoner digs up the body which of course is not dead, and then force-feeds the victim a paste from the Datura plant, known in Haiti as zombie cucumber which causes amnesia and then the victim can be sold as a slave. One victim who had been poisoned many year before by his brother and sold as a slave, returned to Haiti on the death of his owner in 1980.

WHEN DOES DEATH OCCUR?

There have been some conflicting opinions between doctors as to when death actually occurs, when the body has not been so mutilated that there is no question.

When there is excessive brain damage, so that the person is in a coma, and only kept alive by intravenous feeding etc, I think that should constitute death.

But there have been many reports of people pronounced dead and put in hospital mortuaries, who have come back to life. (Most of them have only lived for a few days.)

But there was a young American woman on T.V. who had donated her kidneys, and was pronounced dead, and only came back to life with the first plunge of the knife. If her kidneys had been removed she would indeed have been dead. She is apparently still living.

The Romans, in olden times, were so afraid of being buried alive that burial did not take place until the first signs of decomposition set in. I suppose we should all be buried or cremated with a plastic bag wrapped tightly round our faces so that we would not have the misfortune of recovery after burial or during cremation.